PRAISE FOR *THE BIG FISH EXPERIENCE*

No matter what level you're at today, *The Big Fish Experience* will help you take it up a notch—to deliver to your audiences the experiences they've always dreamed about.

—Dave Kerpen, *New York Times* bestselling author of *The Art of People* and international keynote speaker

In today's high-stakes business world, it's not uncommon for one presentation to be a make-it-or-break-it opportunity. Whether you're preparing for a multimillion-dollar pitch or just want to ace a presentation, *The Big Fish Experience* offers smart, actionable tips to help every presenter take his or her presentation to the next level.

—Brittany Hodak, cofounder of ZinePak and winner of *Shark Tank*

The Big Fish Experience will help entrepreneurs and those with big ideas tell their stories in a more captivating and visual way than ever before. Definitely recommend this book to presenters looking for resources, tools, and ideas on how to make an impact with the audience.

—Scott Gerber, founder of YEC and author of *Never Get a "Real" Job*

Being an entrepreneur means that I often have to invite employees, advisors, investors, and customers to support and share my vision. I have learned that speaking in front of an audience of several hundred people requires more than confidence. Presenters must have a plan for developing their message, sharing it in a compelling way, and using tools to present captivating visual elements that support one's arguments. In *The Big Fish Experience*, Kenny, Gus, Rob, and Luke take you through the entire process of planning, creating, and delivering presentations that will inform and inspire any audience.

—David Hassell, CEO of 15Five

This book will help any presenter reimagine how presentations should be in this death-by-PowerPoint-filled world.

—Javier Farfan, VP of segment and cultural marketing at Verizon

Good presenters aren't magically created, they are made with lots of empathy, consideration for their audience, and hard work. This book perfectly encapsulates what separates the run-of-the-mill from the truly exceptional.

—Sean Blanda, director and editor in chief of 99u

Big Fish offers a unique presentation style guide personalized for any user with simple, practical tips and tricks to elevate the presentation experience.

—Stephen Burns, global aerospace segment leader at Kimberly-Clark Corporation

This is absolutely one of the more helpful and actionable public speaking books on the market. The advice is authentic and can help anyone from newcomers to veterans enhance their skill set to comfortably command a stage.

—Sarah Bedrick, certifications program leader at HubSpot

In these pages, you will learn how to move from being a presenter to becoming a true storyteller.

—Andres Traslavina, global recruiting manager at Whole Foods Market

Everyone should read this book before your next big pitch.

—Tim Williamson, CEO of Idea Village

Unleash your inner TED talk.

—Josh Koppel, founder of Scrollmotion

Like its authors, *The Big Fish Experience* is bold, forward-thinking, inspiring, and utterly engaging. If you've ever delivered a boring presentation (and who among us hasn't?), this book will show you that there is a better way. You'll get the tools and inspiration you need to go from mind-numbing to mind-blowing. You owe it to your audiences—and to yourself—to read this book.

—Amy Stevens, AVP of marketing and communication at Tidelands Health

The Big Fish Experience lays out a logical, effective road map for developing enhanced storytelling for corporate presentations.

—Scott Collignon, senior director of supply chain operations at Cabela's

A true Presenting 101! In these pages, you will learn how to create a memorable experience for your audience.

—**Frank Marino, VP of marketing at Atmos Energy**

Given the competitive nature of today's advertising business, it is essential for our sales team to deliver the best presentations among peer media reps. Big Fish Presentations offers practical, insightful tips to design effective, powerful presentations. This is required reading for design teams or anyone who wants to create a standout presentation.

—**Mendi Robinson, creative director at Lamar Advertising Company**

The Big Fish Experience explores in depth every essential part of a great presentation experience. Best of all, it does it in an approachable way—with plenty of real examples.

—**Chanda D. Leary-Coutu, senior manager of marketing communications at Wellpet**

I would've loved to read this book before I started my professional speaking career. It is comprehensive, fun, and filled with engaging stories that link the concepts of effective presentations to powerful delivery. It is ideal for both beginners and expert presenters.

—**Dima Ghawi, TEDx talker and founder of Breaking Vases**

If you feel like you're not challenging yourself enough in public speaking, pick up this book.

—**Jeremey Donovan, bestselling author of *How to Deliver a TED Talk* and *Speaker, Leader, Champion***

The team behind Big Fish Presentations really understands how to make presentations that impress. Their philosophy of approaching it like a top chef makes sense. What you need are great ingredients (content), flawless technique (design), and presentation (powerful delivery). The result is a feast for your audience that will take you to the top of your field.

—**Sonia Arrison, author of *100 Plus***

THE
BIGFISH
EXPERIENCE

CREATE MEMORABLE PRESENTATIONS
THAT REEL IN YOUR AUDIENCE

KENNY NGUYEN · GUS MURILLO · ROBERT KILLEEN · LUKE JONES

NEW YORK   CHICAGO   SAN FRANCISCO   ATHENS
LONDON   MADRID   MEXICO CITY   MILAN
NEW DELHI   SINGAPORE   SYDNEY   TORONTO

1 2 3 4 5 6 7 8 9 0   DOW/DOW   1 2 1 0 9 8 7 6 5

ISBN 978-0-07-183492-6
MHID   0-07-183492-3

e-ISBN 978-0-07-183493-3
e-MHID   0-07-183493-1

Library of Congress Cataloging-in-Publication Data

Names: Nguyen, Kenny. | Murillo, Gus. | Killeen, Robert.
Title: The big fish experience : create memorable presentations that reel in
   your audience / by Kenny Nguyen, Gus Murillo, Robert Killeen and Luke Jones.
Description: New York : McGraw-Hill Education, 2016.
Identifiers: LCCN 2015031167| ISBN 9780071834926 (paperback : alk. paper) |
   ISBN 0071834923
Subjects: LCSH: Business presentations. | Business communication. | BISAC:
   BUSINESS & ECONOMICS / Business Communication / Meetings & Presentations.
Classification: LCC HF5718.22 .N49 2016 | DDC 658.4/52--dc23 LC record available at
   http://lccn.loc.gov/   2015031167

McGraw-Hill Education books are available at special quantity discounts to use as premiums and sales promotions or for use in corporate training programs. To contact a representative, please visit the Contact Us pages at www.mhprofessional.com.

To Kelsie, Sofia, Gus, Evelyn, and Tracey

Kevin, Khoi, Mary, and Laura

Sarah, will you marry me?

Albus

CONTENTS

OUR STORY

In January 2011, we (Kenny Nguyen and Gus Murillo) experienced the most boring presentation of our lives while watching a Fortune 500 executive speak at a student organization function. Sitting there completely miserable, faced with a presentation that consisted of hundreds of slides with nothing but text, we had this crazy idea to create a company that would rid the world of boring presentations.

Big Fish Presentations was born. We started out helping small clients, "small fish," present like "big fish" in a vast ocean of competition.

Today, Big Fish Presentations is a leading visual and video production firm; our clients range from start-ups to Fortune 500 companies. We work with brands that want to present themselves in new and innovative ways while keeping design, communication, and effective delivery in mind. Whether it is by designing a high-quality slide deck, training entrepreneurs for a $2-million pitch, or producing a 30-second video showcasing a company's brand to the public, Big Fish strives to transform each presentation into an experience for the audience.

ACKNOWLEDGMENTS

I'm going to get really cheesy here. After all, it's not every day you get to write a book for your dream publisher and work with the most amazing team in the world.

So in the spirit of appreciation, I'd like to thank a number of folks who have been instrumental in not only writing the book you are reading now but achieving the overall success of Big Fish Presentations.

(*Disclaimer:* There are hundreds of people who are responsible for helping build Big Fish. For the sake of saving trees and attention spans, I couldn't possibly thank each of them by name in the pages of this book. I'll be sure to thank them personally, though.)

To the Big Fish Presentations team: You are my heroes. You make coming to work every day worth it. Big Fish wouldn't be possible without you, and I can't wait to see what the future holds for us. The long nights in the office and weekend work don't seem so bad when the time is spent with company as great as yours. I look forward to working with you throughout the years.

To the McGraw-Hill team: Thank you for believing in us. It was an unreal experience when Casey Ebro reached out to us with the opportunity to write the book we've always wanted to write. We've given it our all. Thank you for allowing us to be us. During a Big Fish visit to New York, I stood with the team right in front of the McGraw-Hill offices and told the guys that one day we would write a book for you. While I was being ambitious, I never thought that in two weeks we would receive an e-mail from you, asking us to "capture our lightning in a bottle" and share it with the world! Thank you for the opportunity. We hope you are pleased with our work.

To the team that provided valuable feedback: Janae Bourgeois, Sarah Bedrick, Dima Ghawi, and Big Gus, thank you for giving us the reassurance and constructive criticism to take this book to the next level.

To all our clients: Thank you for believing in us. We know that with every presentation, a lot is on the line. Thank you for trusting us with your future success. We never take that for granted, and we value our relationships with you very deeply. Expect even greater things from us. We're always striving to improve ourselves and are looking forward to helping you spread your message even more powerfully than before.

To my father, Kevin Nguyen: Thank you for encouraging me to follow my dream and take a different route. Without that encouragement, my pen never would have hit the paper to begin writing this book. You've pushed me beyond my limits and challenged me throughout my life. I have nothing but appreciation for the sacrifices you have made for our family. I hope this book will be a symbol of all the hard work you've put into raising me.

To my business partner and Gus's father, Gus Murillo: Thank you for being a mentor and also our first client. Your purchase of the first Big Fish presentation was life-changing. You helped craft an idea that led to this book. Your continued support as my sales mentor has been indispensable, and I value our relationship very much. I hope we continue to grow and work together throughout the years.

To my best friend and business partner, Gus Murillo: We are living the dream, man! I couldn't imagine doing a venture with anyone else but you. You've always been like a brother to me, and we are very lucky to be among the few people who can be best friends *and* start a business together. Our friendship and partnership are among what I cherish most in my life, and I look forward to continuing to build this company together.

To the reader: You have no idea what this means to the Big Fish Presentations team and me. You are reading five years' worth of our work, helping clients all over the world deliver experiences for their audiences. Thank you for helping us get to where we are today. We hope that we can help you deliver the most amazing presentations you never thought you'd be able to give. Please tell us how this book has affected you, good or bad. We will listen and constantly strive for improvement. E-mail us at hq@bigfishpresentations.com, and we'll get back to you.

We can never adequately thank the people who have contributed to our success. We hope this book will help you achieve your dreams.

Here's to presenting experiences far and wide,

Kenny Nguyen
CEO and cofounder of

HOW TO USE THIS BOOK

We know you're busy.

In order to maximize your time, here are some tips to help you get the most out of this book.

Write Down Your Goals

Write down 10 goals that you wish to accomplish to become a better presenter. Why 10? Well, because we like to keep it simple. Too many may overwhelm you, and too few may not challenge you. We want you to become the best presenter you can be. To help with your goals, at the end of each chapter, we suggest challenges based on the content. The key is to share these goals with trusted friends, family members, and coworkers and have them hold you accountable for meeting them. We understand that everyone is at a different presentation skill level, so we tiered the challenges to push even the best presenters out of their comfort zone.

Here are some sample goals:

1. Deliver my next presentation without a PowerPoint deck.

2. Deliver my next presentation without note cards.

3. Create my next presentation with fewer than 10 words on every slide.

If you accomplish all your goals, please let us know at hq@bigfishpresentations.com!

If You Feel as If You Already Know the Material in a Chapter, Don't Be Afraid to Skip Ahead

This book was built for all levels of presenters. That's why we summarize what we cover at the beginning of each chapter. This way, if you feel that you're already comfortable with a certain topic, you can challenge yourself by moving on to a section farther ahead.

For those in a rush for quick advice: In the back of this book, the section "Extra Resources" lists the key points in each chapter. While we suggest reading the whole book, these salient points should come in handy as you prepare your presentation, to remind yourself of what you may have missed or need to refine.

Keep on the Lookout for a Life Preserver with a K on It

Whenever you see an image of a life preserver with a K in the middle, you'll find personal tips from Kenny on keynote speaking and coaching.

Practice What You Read in Front of People Regularly

Just reading this book won't make you a great presenter. You have to practice. Schedule practice sessions on any topic with your coworkers, bosses, professors, friends, or family members to try out new techniques. Great communication takes practice. For this book to make a difference in your life, the secret is to practice so much that it begins to feel natural. When good habits become natural, you can focus on improving other presentation techniques.

Do Not Be Afraid to Try Something New

Presentations are constantly evolving. There might be some material in these pages that may not resonate with you. That's OK. Just keep an open mind. Be receptive to trying new things with the mission to become a better presenter today than you were yesterday. Be bold. Go out there and try something new. Your audience will respect you for it.

Keep Learning

If there are any new creative ways you see presenters use to engage their audience that we have not discussed here but that you would love for us to write about on our blog, Hookyouraudience.com, please e-mail us at hq@bigfishpresentations.com. We would love to hear from you!

DESIGN

CONTENT

THE BIG FISH PRESENTATIONS PROCESS

DELIVERY

WHAT DEFINES AN EXPERIENCE?

Plans are of little importance, but planning is essential.

—WINSTON CHURCHILL

When you hear the word "experience," what comes to mind? A concert where people are screaming their lungs out? A sporting event where fans are cheering for their team? A performance by a group like Cirque du Soleil?

All these definitely would qualify as an experience because all offer something more than just music, sports, and entertainment. Each is a memorable event that people will cherish and relive in their thoughts. Have you ever considered that a presentation also could qualify as an experience?

We don't commonly associate the word "presentation" with the euphoria of a concert or ball game. If a presentation is ever thought of as an experience, it is probably considered a bad one. Very rarely do you hear the word "memorable" or "exciting" to describe a presentation. We usually only hear that in connection to Apple product launches or TED talks. Great presenters who deliver amazing experiences account for just 1 percent of all presenters. What about the remaining 99 percent?

These presenters have three major problems. First, many rely too much on their software rather than build trust with the audience. Second, they do not prepare adequately to meet the demands of the attention spans of today's audiences. Last, presenters do not take the time to understand what their audiences really want.

The result? Audiences have become so numb from bad presenters, that *they're actually surprised to see a good one.*

We at Big Fish Presentations want you to join the 1 percent, and our aim is for those ranks to grow.

In the next section, you'll learn about our battle-tested, three-step process for creating a great presentation. Learning and applying the process will be your first step in getting your audience to believe in you.

CIRCQUE DU SOLEIL

"Quidam," 2011
Randy Miramontez/Shutterstock.com

OUR PROCESS

ENGAGING CONTENT + MEMORABLE AND SIMPLE VISUALS + POWERFUL DELIVERY = UNFORGETTABLE EXPERIENCE

While this might seem simple, it actually took years to create and fine-tune this complex process. This book is structured to simulate the way we think when building a presentation from the ground up. We go from nailing down a solid concept, to incorporating visuals, and finally to working on strong execution. Having a clear process to follow makes the entire presentation experience more enjoyable and memorable.

As the equation indicates, this is a three-step process:

1. *Engaging content.* Creating engaging content provides the foundation and the call to action for the presentation. Content is king in the presentation world. Focus your efforts on developing the most engaging story and vision possible to get your listeners invested in what you have to say. You need them to be able to understand your message to believe in it.

2. *Memorable and simple design.* If content is the king of the presentation, then design is the queen. It's easier to make a beautiful slide deck when you have a strong foundation and vision. Consider your presentation aesthetic and think about how your design connects with the audience. Focus on the relationship between your listeners' hearts and minds rather than just trying to make a slide that "looks nice." Design with an outcome in mind.

3. *Powerful delivery,* This is the final step in presenting a message that can create change. Strong body language, confidence, and connection are key. Well-designed presentations are important, but there is no replacement for the most important differentiator: *you!* People will always remember the presenter more than the presentation. Presenters are the difference makers; they hold the power to persuade.

In this book, you will learn what it takes to master each step in detail. But before going deeper into our process, we'd like to introduce our 10 commandments.

Kenny's Tip

Before founding the company, I trained for a couple of years to become a chef. While learning how to create dishes that would wow the patrons at my uncle's restaurant, I discovered the components of a life-changing meal: great ingredients, flawless technique, and presentation.

Creating presentations is very similar to creating a great meal.

GREAT INGREDIENTS = GREAT CONTENT

FLAWLESS TECHNIQUE = HIGH-QUALITY DESIGN

PRESENTATION = POWERFUL DELIVERY

While both a great presentation and a great meal require the proper atmosphere to be delivered effectively, if executed properly, both can result in a life-changing experience for the recipient. Think of the greatest meal you've ever had when creating your presentation. Think of all the elements that made the meal memorable and how it made you feel. In the same way, we remember the most powerful presentations we've witnessed in our lives.

THE BIG FISH PRESENTATIONS COMMANDMENTS

Here are our 10 most useful tips in the form of commandments. These are the ideals that form our presentation philosophy. As you make your way through this book, keep them in mind. They will help you become a more personable, well-rounded, and confident presenter.

1. Present what's in it for the world, not you.

2. Remember that time is not a renewable resource; respect it.

3. Never deliver a presentation you wouldn't want to sit through.

4. Be aware that people will always remember the presenter more than the presentation.

5. Be passionate about your topic.

6. Tell stories.

7. Always have a progression that leads to a call to action.

8. If you think you've rehearsed enough, rehearse again.

9. Engage with the audience when possible.

10. Have fun.

We'll elaborate on these commandments in much more detail throughout the book. We believe they can get anyone on the right track to becoming a great presenter.

You are now ready to begin the first step in turning your next presentation into an experience. Get ready to create engaging content that can move your audience.

CONTENT

> *Words have incredible power. They can make people's hearts soar, or they can make people's hearts sore.*
>
> —DR. MARDY GROTHE

The foundation of every presentation is its content. It can have the best transitions, highest-quality pictures, and most intricate, visually stunning design; however, if it says nothing, it will achieve nothing. You're presenting for a reason: you're trying to communicate something. Your content is what your audience is going to latch on to and remember. It's your big idea, your message, your approach.

You're going to be in a roomful of people, with their own opinions and perspectives. You have to make sure that whatever it is you're about to tell them is powerful, entertaining, persuasive, and credible, whether it's meant to educate, inspire, persuade, or move your audience to tears or laughter.

It's not always about what you want to say, as much as what your listeners want to hear. Who are they? What do they like? What's their demographic and psychographic (their values)? The answers to these questions will help mold your content and will make or break your presentation.

If people don't feel that what you're saying is important, they'll zone out. If you're not saying something that interests them, they'll zone out. And even if what you're saying interests them but you're not saying it in a *way* that interests them, they'll zone out. It's a double-edged sword because both what you say and how you say it will determine their attention. Some say that the average audience attention span is five minutes.[1] Unfortunately, it's likely your presentation will be longer than that. You need to make sure that what you're saying captivates your listeners and keeps them engaged.

In this chapter, we'll discuss the following:

- RESEARCH
- THE BIG IDEA
- A SIMPLE CENTRAL MESSAGE
- THE OPENER
- THE STORY

- DATA
- CALL TO ACTION
- STRUCTURE
- LINES THAT STICK
- MAKE ANYTHING INTERESTING

RESEARCH

Research is crucial. Before you buy a house, you do research. Before you go to a job interview, you do research. Before you begin a new initiative at work, you do research. No matter what we do in life, there's always a certain level of research and planning that we do before we act. What's the quickest way to the office? Which vendor offers the lowest prices? What company would I like to work for?

It's no different when it comes to presenting. As a presenter, you need to research your topic and the audience to whom you're speaking. When researching a topic, the first thing you need to understand is that there will never be a point when the research will be complete. Never. There will always be more to learn. The goal isn't to research until you feel as though you've exhausted all the sources. The goal is to research until you can talk about a topic confidently and comfortably. This is important for two reasons: you'll look at your slides less, and you'll be able to answer any questions thrown at you.

Using slides as a crutch can inhibit your credibility as a presenter, so as a rule, don't rely on them. Researching your topic thoroughly ensures you won't have to. This also makes it easier for you to create simpler and more succinct slides, using them only as a guide.

So how do you research a topic well enough to know everything you need to know? Let's say you have to give a presentation on a book, but you have nothing else to go on. You don't know who's in the audience or the point of the presentation. All you know is that you're going to be talking about a certain book for 30 minutes. What's the first step?

These are the six questions you should ask yourself when doing research:

Who?	What?	When?	Where?	Why?	How?

For the purposes of our example, you should ask yourself:

- What is the book about?

- What is its purpose?

- Who is the intended reader?

- Who are the authors?

- What do they do?

- Why did they write it?

It's a brief example, but each of these questions will lead to even more questions. The point is not to simply ask these six questions and be done but to apply them to every single aspect of the topic. Remember:

- There will never be an end point.

- No information is useless.

- Question everything.

- Google is your friend.

What if you are an expert in your subject? Let's say you know the answer to every question anyone could ask you. Research prior to your presentation is still important. It will help you refine what you are speaking about and, most important, will lead you to the second phase of your research.

This involves understanding exactly to whom you are speaking. When you know who your listeners are, you will know what they want to hear and how they want to hear it. This is crucial to any presentation. Once you know your audience, you can understand their needs.

In defining the audience, pay attention to the event itself. It's important to understand the context. Is it a conference with an entry fee? Is this a professional audience? A group of students? Are there other speakers? If so, what are their topics?

Regardless of how you find out information about the audience, the point is to spend time doing so. When you are able to gauge the likes and dislikes of those to whom you're speaking, you can tailor your message to ensure its effectiveness with that particular audience.

You may apply the six questions to researching your audience:

1. Why am I speaking?

2. Who am I speaking to?

3. What does the audience want to hear?

4. How am I going to best satisfy their needs?

5. When am I speaking?

6. Where is the venue/stage/area?

Other questions to ask about your audience:

- Do I have any relevant personal stories to which my target audience can relate?

- What medium (presentation tool) am I going to use to best reach my audience?

- What do I want my listeners to do with the information I give them?

- What do they already know about the topic?

- What are possible questions or objections my topic may raise?

- Is there technical information that may confuse my audience?

- Am I careful not to offend anybody when speaking about controversial issues such as religion, race, or politics?

- If speaking to a foreign audience, am I sure that none of my material can be considered offensive?

Many of us are asked to present at a conference. We know that people aren't going to pay to watch a movie they don't think they'll like. It's the same way with conference presentations. If you know that all the speakers are talking about the same subject, it's a good indication of the audience's interests. When in doubt, just ask the event coordinator. This is, however, not foolproof. There will *always* be members of the audience who are outliers. To hook them, aim to make your presentation interesting in general, regardless of who is listening (more on this later).

This example provides two great lessons for researching your audience. Lesson one: Use your available resources. Through your main contact, identify the

CASE STUDY

A major electronics retailer asked us to help create a pitch to its large clients to invest in the company's new interactive technology. The challenge: multiple target audiences from different departments would influence the final purchasing decision. Within this group of stakeholders were CEOs, marketers, accountants, engineers, and developers, all of whom wanted their needs addressed. If the pitch failed to do this, it would delay future sales.

We tailored our approach. We opened the presentation with common elements related to all the stakeholders, and then we proceeded to address each group's needs while tying in what it meant for the other groups: "With the addition of this technology, your customers will be able to do *X* and experience interactive technology like never before [for the marketers]. While revolutionary, this technology also comes with compatible upgrades to your current technology [for the engineers] without incurring a heavy cost [for the accountants and CEOs who care about the bottom line]." This inclusive approach provided reassurance to every department that its needs would be satisfied.

various groups within and interests of your audience. Ask the necessary questions. Lesson two: In the event of a diverse audience, generalize the message, and then use an inclusive approach to address each group's needs.

Being knowledgeable about a topic is a great way to exude confidence and credibility, and knowing your listeners' needs is the best way to move them.

Don't give a presentation without researching your topic and audience.

Kenny's Tip

Your primary contact (client, event organizer, host, etc.) is your best resource. But use other resources as well. Look up past periodicals geared toward the audience or event, interview members of the past or current audience, or ask previous speakers about their experience with the audience.

THE BIG IDEA

We cannot stress this enough: all presentations need a big idea. *The big idea defines the purpose of the presentation.* It is essentially an argument. It can be inspiring, challenging, or controversial. The big idea is the basis for the content of your entire presentation. It will determine the way you approach your argument, message, overall tone, and the feeling you wish to convey. Behind every great presentation is a big idea. Its importance cannot be underestimated.

We're going to show you how to pick not only a good big idea but the best one.

First, it's important to note that big ideas are not topics. While the topic "how to change your presentation game" might sound interesting, to truly succeed, it needs a big idea, such as "to change your presentation game, you must deliver a presentation you would want to sit through yourself." Big ideas are statements that relate to the topic but also offer a solution that may challenge the audience's way of thinking.

However, a big idea can't be effective on its own. The impact of your big idea depends greatly on the quality of your supporting content and the context in which you are presenting it. In other words, you need to know exactly who the people in your audience are and then give them a reason to believe you.

For example, if you deliver a speech with a big idea to "increase sales by hiring the best talent, training them, and letting them do their work" to a crowd of seasoned sales managers, they probably will tune out because this idea isn't going to change the way they think or feel. However, if you were to propose this big idea to a group of brand-new, inexperienced sales managers, this might be something that opens their eyes. It may be new to them, and it may motivate them to learn more. You are giving them value with your idea.

Another example is Drew Dudley's TEDx talk, "Leading with Lollipops." Dudley didn't state his big idea until the end of his presentation about leadership: "We need to redefine leadership as being about lollipop moments, how many of them we create, how many of

CASE STUDY

In Kenny's TEDx talk, "The Art of Saying No," he told the audience how saying no can lead to future opportunities. He set the stage by recounting the story of how saying no prevented him from injury when he was a child. The subject was established. He needed a way to make people see the words "yes" and "no" with new eyes. This is what his big idea led to: "Today I want you to think of something very differently when it comes to the word 'no.' I want you to think of 'no' as a protective shield in opposition to the sword of 'yes.'" This big idea contained an analogy that allowed his audience to easily remember him and his presentation.

KENNY NGUYEN

TEDx LSU

Big Fish Presentations

them we acknowledge, how many of them we pay forward, and how many of them we say thank you for." This was a powerful call to action that was delivered after a story about a lady who thanked him for breaking the ice between her and a classmate (spoiler alert: they ended up getting married). He moved his listeners and then called upon them to act on his big idea.

The big idea of this book is: *to be among the top 1 percent of presenters, one must take on the ambitious goal to make each presentation an experience for the audience by combining engaging content, memorable and simple visuals, and powerful delivery.*

Remember, it's better to focus on one powerful idea than multiple ideas. You want to rally the audience around a central idea. Always choose quality over quantity. Having too many big ideas can distract your audience and dilute your message.

Here are some examples of famous TED talks that focus on one big idea backed up by solid content (you'll find the big idea in italics):

MELLODY HOBSON, "Color Blind or Color Brave":

So I think it's time for us to be comfortable with the uncomfortable conversation about race: black, white, Asian, Hispanic, male, female, all of us, if we truly believe in equal rights and equal opportunity in America, I think we have to have real conversations about this issue. *We cannot afford to be color blind. We have to be color brave. We have to be willing, as teachers and parents and entrepreneurs and scientists, we have to be willing to have proactive conversations about race with honesty and understanding and courage, not because it's the right thing to do, but because it's the smart thing to do, because our businesses and our products and our science, our research, all of that will be better with greater diversity.*

CHRIS HADFIELD, "What I Learned from Going Blind in Space":

. . . looking at the difference between perceived danger and actual danger, where is the real risk? What is the real thing that you should be afraid of? Not just a generic fear of bad things happening. *You can fundamentally change your reaction to things so that it allows you to go places and see things and do things that otherwise would be completely denied to you . . .*

SHAWN ACHOR, "The Happy Secret to Better Work":

And the problem is it's scientifically broken and backwards for two reasons. Every time your brain has a success, you just changed the goalpost of what success looked like. You got good grades, now you have to get better grades; you got into a good school and after you get into a better one; you got a good job, now you have to get a better job; you hit your sales target, we're going to change it. *And if happiness is on the opposite side of success, your brain never gets there. We've pushed happiness over the cognitive horizon, as a society. And that's because we think we have to be successful, then we'll be happier.*

These speakers masterfully captivate and inspire the audience with big ideas that are supported by powerful stories or strong data, which enable the speakers to make more convincing arguments. This is at the core of all great presentations.

Keep in mind that the presenters may not have revealed their big ideas at the same point in their talk. If you structure your talk well and use the tenets of storytelling, the unveiling of the big idea will be the moment that your audience feels emotionally challenged.

The big idea does not just state your thesis; it inspires and creates action. Boiling down your message into one simple idea means reaching deep down into your topic and pulling out what matters most. Only then can you truly touch the hearts and minds of your audience. Remember, everything that's ever been achieved started from a single idea.

A SIMPLE CENTRAL MESSAGE

A common problem in presentations, or communication in general, is the lack of simplicity. All too often we see PowerPoint slides that are brimming with text. This is due to the presenter's inability to simplify his or her message. Most presenters fear they will fail to convey their idea, so they provide as much elaboration and information as possible to ensure that the audience gets it. However, this accomplishes the opposite: it overwhelms people to the extent that they zone out.

We get it. In introducing a new service or training, it needs to be explained in detail, but the answer isn't to fill each slide with a wall of text. The answer is to simplify your message. This is crucial in every aspect of a presentation, not just the content. It's common sense: complex ideas are hard to understand, and simple ideas are easy to understand. Why say something in 20 words when you can say it in 7? Why include all the colors when you can pick just two? Why talk about the extra details that aren't important? Whether it's with content, design, or delivery, simplifying every aspect of your presentation is a good thing. If your content is simple, it is easier to understand and remember. The simpler the design, the more cohesive and effective the presentation. If your delivery is simple, you'll come off as natural and confident in a way that connects with your audience.

Give your listeners some credit. Don't insult them by holding their hand and walking them through every slide. Allow them to come to their own conclusions.

How?

If You Can't Say What Your Presentation Is About in One Sentence, You're Doing Something Wrong

The best way to simplify a message is to say it in a single sentence. How is that possible? Easy. When our clients aren't sure what their overall message is, we often ask them that if they could express it in only one sentence, what would it be? This forces them to uncover the simplest version of their idea and to realize the importance of brevity. Once you're able to boil down your presentation into a single sentence, build every slide around that one idea to ensure your message is prevalent throughout. This one sentence is the main takeaway for your audience.

How is this different from your big idea? Well, your central message is the content that helps the audience understand the big idea more clearly. Your big idea is a challenge to the audience; your central message is a simple way to express it.

Explain Like I'm Five

This simple advice will help you get rid of the jargon, clutter, and dead weight of your presentation material to reveal the underlying message. The next time you're preparing for a presentation, ask one of your friends to be your audience while you do a practice run. However, instead of viewing him (or her) as your friend, pretend he's a child. If you put too much text on a slide, he won't read it. If you give him too much information, jargon, or complexity, he'll become confused. And if your message isn't simple, he'll forget what you said. You can lose your audience at any moment unless your message is the simplest version of itself.

The hardest part is sticking to this rule. We're not always allowed to pick our topic, the subject we present, or the amount of information we have to throw at the audience. However, it's important to remember that *you can simplify content without omitting information.* The next time you need help condensing information, just pretend you have to present to a group of five-year-olds.

It's about focusing on the bigger picture, the message you want your audience to walk away with. What is it? What do you want people to be thinking when they get up and leave? They're not going to remember how the pillars of your company are structured on that one slide with all the stats. They're going to remember the theme of your presentation, the message it conveyed to them—or they're going to remember nothing at all. Don't bury the audience with explanations, elaborations, examples, and so on, when none are actually needed. If the purpose of slide 13 is to help explain slide 12, then slide 12 isn't good enough.

We've successfully taken 200-slide presentations and reduced them to a single idea, so we can say unequivocally that there are no exceptions to refining your message. You just need to look over everything you have, remove the complexity, and focus on the main points. After you've done that, combine those points into a single sentence and build your presentation from there. Make your message known on every slide, but leave enough mystery for your listeners to bridge the gaps themselves. You want them to move along easily, and that's possible only with simple information.

Let's say a shoe company has hundreds of different types of athletic shoes—a shoe for every sport, activity, or hobby. And it has all these types of shoes because it wants its customers to feel confident in every area of activity they do currently or may want to do in the future.

However, when the company presents its message—its idea—it doesn't show every shoe and explain every shoe's function. It doesn't list all the values the company is built on or the profit margins that show it's successful, followed by a few testimonials and case studies. All it says is a single, simple sentence that even a five-year-old can understand:

Just do it.

THE OPENER

There is only one excuse for a speaker's asking the attention of his audience: he must have either truth or entertainment for them.

—DALE CARNEGIE, *The Art of Public Speaking*

Getting your audience's attention is a tricky thing. At the beginning of any presentation, some say you have only seven seconds to make a good first impression.[2] Once that moment passes and people perceive you as boring or irrelevant, it will be nearly impossible to pique their curiosity again. You will spend the rest of your presentation in an uphill battle, desperately trying to regain their attention. This is something that you cannot afford to do. A presentation is essentially a pitch, so if you initially lose your listeners and then somehow hook them back, the effect will still not be as powerful as it could have been.

You can prevent this quite easily if you're prepared. Your presentation begins as soon as you walk onstage. Smile and appear warm and friendly. Your opening lines set the tone for your overall performance, so preparing a great intro primes your listeners for the message they're about to receive. If they are entertained in the first few minutes, then they're more likely to be excited about your message and therefore to remember it later. That's the end goal, right? To make an impact and instill an idea within someone in order to create change. To do that, you've got to start with a bang.

Easier said than done. It's not as simple as throwing out an inspiring quote, fact, or statement. The opener has to give the audience a brief glimpse into the rest of the presentation. It's your window of opportunity. How do you grab and keep your audience's attention?

Kenny's Tip

Before your presentation, it's good practice to introduce yourself to members of the audience. This creates allies. Ask them what they are most excited about in the presentation and what they would most like to learn. The goal is to have the audience get to know you as a speaker who authentically cares about their interests.

Stories

Everyone loves a good story. We all have our own. Telling a story is sharing an experience with your listeners that temporarily transports them to a world of your making that enables them to identify with you. In that moment, everyone who's listening is in the same place experiencing a small adventure together. A bond is created. You have established a connection with your audience that gives you the opportunity to share your message. This is probably the most effective opener, yet the hardest. The key is to make sure the story isn't so specific that you lose some people, just specific enough to be relatable to everyone. For example, when Kenny opens a pitch presentation to a client, he begins with the origin story of Big Fish Presentations. He tells the audience how he witnessed a bad presentation and swore to do something about it.

Use story openers when you need to connect emotionally with your audience on a personal level. Stories can take a little bit more time to build up, so keep only the details that are necessary and make sure each sentence moves the story along. Otherwise, the audience might start to wander off.

Questions

Kicking off your presentation with a question is a quick, easy way to open up a room and show that you're personable. Not only does it get the audience thinking and talking, but it also works to loosen up the crowd. Everyone is taken out of autopilot mode and nudged into interacting, even if it's just for a few seconds or only a couple of words. It's enough of a burst of energy to prime the audience for your presentation. Make your question specific to the situation. For example, if you are presenting to a group of marine biologists, you wouldn't want to open with a pop culture reference unless you can relate it directly to your presentation. The best option would be to refer to a recent biological discovery with which the audience is likely to be familiar.

Use question openers when you need people to open their minds to new ideas. Asking the audience multiple questions is a great way to get a grasp of your listeners' working knowledge of the material of your presentation.

Quotes

Don't judge each day by the harvest you reap but by the seeds that you plant.

—Robert Louis Stevenson

Using the wise words of others at the start of your presentation is a great way both to inspire your audience and to provide a frame of reference. By imparting a tiny nugget of wisdom to your audience, you build the first layer of credibility, even though you're using someone else's words. This shows that you've done your research and are prepared to share a valuable, relevant, and inspiring message. After all, even the most notable, celebrated scholars cite references when sharing their messages. Why shouldn't you?

Use quote openers when you need an influential figure to validate your upcoming statements. This is best employed when the content of your presentation challenges the audience's way of thinking.

Statistics

Numbers or any other type of data can seem boring in presentations. However, when used correctly, statistics can be very effective in illuminating your topic. The key is to use very clear, accurate, and relevant information. A solid statistic places your incoming message in a concrete, irrefutable, and trusted frame of reference. Data not only bolsters your presentation with a trusted source but also lends credibility to everything you say thereafter. Obviously, you want to be positive that you have your facts straight before you present, but you also need to make sure you use relevant, engaging statements that support your message, not just random facts you think will impress the crowd. Statistics are especially effective when they are surprising or disturbing. Celebrity chef Jamie Oliver opened his TED talk about food with, "Sadly, in the next eighteen minutes when I do our chat, four Americans that are alive will be dead from the food that they eat."

Use statistic openers when an audience needs to be aware of an important issue that can be measured. This is best utilized with analytical types. When using a shocking statistic, make sure to explain where it comes from.

Humor

Humor is extremely powerful when used in the right way. A good laugh can loosen up your audience, making your listeners more receptive to you and your message. Be warned, though. A bad joke can be worse than no joke at all. As always, make sure the joke is relevant to the message and caters to the situation. In his TED talk, "Mystery Box," director J. J. Abrams opened by telling the audience that he would rather be discussing polypeptides than doing a TED talk. The audience roared with laughter and was receptive to Abrams for the rest of his presentation.

Use humorous openers when breaking the ice with a crowd of people who may not be familiar with each other or when trying to find a way to charm the audience with new ideas. Funny stories or jokes pertinent to the content of your presentation are highly effective—but risky because not every audience member may get the punch line.

Video and Photography

While promoting *The 4-Hour Body*, bestselling author Tim Ferriss released an incredible book trailer (which received over a million views) that gave fans details about what to expect and pump them up for a new lifestyle change. He incorporated a version of this

Kenny's Tip

Humor is a very difficult presentation skill to master. From my experience, self-deprecating humor in the form of stories is a good way to win over a crowd because it makes you sympathetic.

If the audience is lively and I've made some friends beforehand, I'll sometimes open with a funny experience that occurred in the audience's city (even better if I can relate the story to my topic or the theme of the event).

I once wore a black turtleneck and jeans to a presentation. Right before I began, I realized that I looked like an Asian Steve Jobs! I opened my presentation by saying that I knew who I looked like, and I whipped out my iPad mini and introduced it as the iPhone 6 plus plus. The audience roared with laughter. Humor made me instantly likable.

trailer into the opening of his presentation for South by Southwest and got the audience really excited to see more. If you're thinking of using video or photography at the beginning of your presentation, make sure it helps evoke emotion and is relevant to the rest of your

I want to start today and talk about the structure of polypeptides.

—J. J. ABRAMS

Producer/Writer of Lost *and* Mission Impossible III

presentation. You don't have to be a famous author or have a big-budget trailer for your presentation, but by taking advantage of those first few moments with cinema, you can make the experience exponentially better. However, don't let a video go on for too long, or the audience will start to get impatient. The longer it is, the harder it will be for the audience to refocus. Keep it to 45–60 seconds for an opener.

Use video and photography openers to evoke emotion and set the tone for the rest of the presentation.

Props

Opening with a physical object that relates to your subject matter is a powerful way for audiences to better visualize your message. An example of this is Bruce Aylward's TED talk, "How We'll Stop Polio for Good." Aylward held a small bottle containing the polio vaccine when asking the audience to think of technology that can change the world.

It's important to note that you don't want to overdo it with your prop throughout the presentation; it can become a distraction to the audience. Either put it away or put it in the background as a subtle reminder to the audience. As long as the prop is introduced with a powerful message, it will be effective.

————

Every aspect of a presentation is important in its own respect, but think of the opener as your first step in its execution. Decide which approach you'd like to practice, master it, and make it your own. You will appear more natural and fluid in your performance.

Quick tip: Having trouble picking an opener for your talk? Try writing it *after* you have all your content for the rest of the presentation. Go ahead and build your presentation structure, including transitions, audience interactions, and a call to action. Then create an opener that reflects this. Although this may sound counterintuitive, it makes your story come full circle and your overall presentation more cohesive.

THE STORY

Ever heard the tale of David and Goliath?

Thousands of years ago, there was a battle between two tribes: the faith-led Israelites and the prideful Philistines. As the battle wore on, the Israelites, led by a man named Saul, grew increasingly troubled. The Philistines had as their hero and champion a giant named Goliath.

Goliath was rumored to stand nine feet tall. For the last 40 days, he had been issuing a challenge to the weary Israelites for a champion to fight him in single combat. This would decide the outcome of the entire battle. While it was an enticing offer, Saul and his people were afraid. No one wanted to accept Goliath's challenge. The Israelites were losing what had made them so strong in the first place, their faith.

Things looked grim for the Israelites until a young boy named David came forward. This young shepherd was bringing food to his famished brothers and heard Goliath's challenge. Confident that anything can be done with faith, David asked Saul if he could be the champion of the Israelites. Although Saul was against the idea, he was out of options. Everyone else was too afraid. He had to put his trust in the young boy.

Armed with faith and a slingshot, David accepted the challenge, much to the Philistines' surprise. They thought, "Are the Israelites so desperate and afraid that they would send a boy?" Goliath, seeing victory in plain sight, relentlessly mocked David and his people.

David, undeterred by the mockery, did not falter. Stepping back, David put the strength of his faith in God into his slingshot. Then he let the rock fly—right at Goliath's head.

At first, nothing happened. The Philistines didn't believe that a small rock could ever topple their hero. But then—thud!

Goliath went down, showing that faith and courage can overpower even the biggest of giants. After the defeat of their hero, the Philistines quickly fled.

This biblical story of David and Goliath has been passed down for generations and adapted multiple times; its emotional power remains.

These classic stories are powerful because they enable us to relate to and sympathize with characters we love, and they teach us life lessons in an emotional and enjoyable way.

This is the true power of stories.

Think of how some of the greatest individuals and organizations in recent history have used stories to impact society:

- Malala Yousafzai draws from her life experiences to fight for girls' education. She has inspired young women all over the world to seek an education.

- Martin Luther King Jr. used inspirational stories of an ideal future to fight for racial equality. His life story hastened the passage of civil rights for all.

- Steve Jobs used stories to explain how Apple products can improve people's lives. His stories inspired entrepreneurs all over the world to make the world a better place.

- Walt Disney founded a movie studio, a company that told stories on the big screen. His way of sharing stories has influenced our generation's most brilliant filmmakers and storytellers.

- J. K. Rowling wrote *Harry Potter*, fantasy fiction that has moved people all over the world to enjoy reading and further explore their imagination.

What makes a good story? There are three elements:

1. The emotional content and context of the story

2. The hero and the villain

3. The suspense

The Emotional Content and Context of the Story

To tell a story properly, first identify its *emotional content and context.*

Think about the most memorable presentations you have ever seen. How did the presenter use stories to:

- Entertain the audience?

- Raise awareness of a cause?

- Present data in a relevant way?

- Make complex topics more comprehensible?

- Inspire an audience to take action?

Appealing to emotions enables a presenter to connect more powerfully—and more memorably—with an audience.

Take, for example, the story of the Texas-based Cody Stephens Foundation (full disclosure: the founders are friends of ours). Its mission is to raise awareness among those at risk of sudden cardiac arrest. The foundation helps Texas school districts implement an electrocardiogram screening program, provide physicals for middle and high school student athletes, and educate young, healthy students about sudden cardiac death.

Think about how a novice presenter and an expert presenter might ask for a donation.

NOVICE PRESENTER

Do you know what sudden cardiac death (SCD) is? It's when the heart suddenly stops doing its job, and the victim goes into cardiac arrest. According to statistics, it's the number one cause of nonaccidental deaths among student athletes. Even more shocking, 1.6 percent of all student athletes have an unknown heart condition that can lead to SCD. But it's preventable. People are not born with it, and it's not due to the blockage of an artery. All you need is an electrocardiogram (ECG) to detect it. Our foundation helps schools in Texas get low-cost ECGs for student athletes. We hope that you will consider donating to prevent future cases of SCD among student athletes.

Great information, but how can we make an audience care at a deeper level? Especially if a person has never been a student athlete or known anyone afflicted with SCD.

Let's give the expert presenter a shot at the story.

EXPERT PRESENTER

On May 6, 2012, Cody Stephens was a few weeks from graduating from Crosby High School and

(continued)

looking forward to showing his pig, steer, and lamb at the Crosby Fair and Rodeo in June. He was excited to be on his way to Tarleton State University on a football scholarship and was working hard to stay in good physical condition.

At 6 feet 9 inches and 289 pounds, he was the image of perfect health. That Sunday afternoon, Cody came home, said he was tired, kicked back in his dad's recliner, and dozed off for a nap. Cody never woke up. He died in his sleep from an ailment called sudden cardiac arrest (SCA). This was something that his family had never heard of. They had no idea that young, seemingly healthy children could be at risk, with relatively few or no warning signs.

Sudden cardiac death (SCD) is the number one cause of nonaccidental deaths among student athletes. Even more shocking, 1.6 percent of all student athletes have an unknown heart condition that can lead to SCD.

Cody's death could have been prevented. People are not born with SCA, and it's not due to the blockage of an artery. All you need is an electrocardiogram (ECG) to detect it. This foundation was created in Cody's honor to prevent deaths from SCA. We help schools in Texas get low-cost ECGs for student athletes. We couldn't save Cody. But we hope you will consider donating to help us save other children.

Of these two, it's easy to see that the second presentation is more powerful. While it's obvious to the listeners that SCD is an important issue, it's very difficult for them to relate, unless they personally know someone who suffered from it. Telling Cody's story makes it relatable. *It's emotional content.* That's the magical effect of merging stories and statistics. When someone takes a global view and brings it to a human level, it's easier to relate and understand. The people in the audience may never have encountered SCD, but after hearing the second presenter speak, they most likely want to help prevent this condition from killing other athletes.

HOW TO BUILD EMOTIONAL CONTEXT

- *Speak about personal experiences that your audience will understand and relate to, that are relevant to their lives.* This will require research on audience demographics.

For example: If Kenny were speaking to a group of worried presenters about the fear of public speaking, he could tell a story about the first time he had to address a large audience. He could describe just how scared he was and how he overcame his fear and gave a good speech. This will make his listeners feel like they are not alone.

- *If presenting data, connect the dots between the topic and the audience.* Identify how your content directly relates to the people in your audience, how it affects them. If it doesn't directly relate to them, find a way to humanize your topic by creating a scenario showing how it could affect them. If it's for a cause, make sure you state the best- and worst-case scenarios.

  For example: Let's say you were fund-raising for a nonprofit that helps rebuild homes after natural disasters. If you were speaking to people interested in donating, a great way to provide a scope of impact is to say, "We have received over $1 million in funding from the community this year. This has enabled us to assist 40 families to rebuild their homes. A total of 200 displaced people now have homes. With your contribution of [dollar amount], you will be able to help [number of] people. In return, this will reduce [positive effect, such as crime rate or homelessness]."

- *Spark the audience's imagination.* Be descriptive in your storytelling. Set the scene (the time you first met a significant other or your best friend). Describe the physical setting, along with every feeling and emotion. Recount the day, the weather, the sounds, even the smells at the time. The more senses you can trigger through your story, the more powerful the audience's reaction.

- *Tell jokes.* A good laugh can release the tension in a room. One of the best ways to warm up the audience is to be funny; crack a joke, make an ironic statement, or tell an embarrassing story. Self-deprecating humor is best. It also doesn't hurt to know a few people in the audience who are good for a sure laugh. After all, laughter is contagious.

While creating great content is critical to swaying the heart, the *proper context* determines the extent to which your audience's heart will open. Think about it: if you were at a fun picnic and someone told you a sad story, wouldn't you think, "Wow, thanks for bringing this to my attention, but couldn't you have done this at a better time?" Context is key. The effectiveness of your story depends on when, where, and how it's delivered.

Kenny's Tip

When we say "how it's delivered," we mean through physical and vocal actions that match your emotional content. Can you imagine hearing an amazing story told in monotone? I didn't think so. Beyond sharing interesting content, great storytellers incorporate pauses, voice inflections, and hand gestures when sharing tales.

The Hero and the Villain

A great story always has great characters: *the hero and the villain*.

The Hero

The hero is the main character of the story who is fighting for something that is for the benefit of the audience. In developing your hero, find out your target audience's values. Find out what they want, what they need, what drives them, and if they have experienced feelings similar to that of your hero. This will help them connect emotionally to your hero.

If you are telling a story that is meant to compel the audience to do something afterward, it is important that they:

1. Relate to your hero

2. Understand what to do next (call to action)

3. Are reminded constantly of what's in it for them, and the world, if the hero succeeds

A good business story's takeaway is this: if the hero succeeds by the audience doing X (this can be as simple as making a purchase or spreading a message), then the world gets Y (your company's main benefit to the world).

The Villain

Every hero needs a worthy villain. Whether it's Goliath or a dangerous ailment such as SCA, the villain is the "problem" in the story. Your job as a storyteller is to show your audience the severity of the problem(s) your hero has to overcome and make them care about *why* your hero needs to defeat the villain. The level of severity will depend on what's at stake in the story.

The audience should feel connected with both the hero and the villain. As the storyteller, it's your task to lay out the possibilities between the problem (the villain) and the solution (the hero), address the confrontation between the two, and pose a potential resolution for *both* sides.

Without a villain to overcome, the audience has no motivation to achieve a goal. Your villain must constantly challenge the success of the hero and your audience. If your villain is a pushover who could be eliminated without the audience's help, they may actually turn on you and feel as if their time has been wasted.

A terrific example is taken from Steve Jobs's address at the 1983 Apple Sales Conference, at which he introduced the infamous Super Bowl "1984" ad and revealed the Macintosh:

> 1983. Apple and IBM emerge as the industry's strongest competitors, each selling approximately $1 billion worth of personal computers in 1983. Each will invest greater than $50 million for R&D and another $50 million for television advertising in 1984, totaling almost one-quarter of a billion dollars combined.
>
> The shakeout is in full swing. The first major firm goes bankrupt, with others teetering on the brink. Total industry losses for 1983 outshadow even the combined profits of Apple and IBM for personal computers.
>
> It is now 1984. It appears IBM wants it all. Apple is perceived to be the only hope to offer IBM a run for its money. Dealers, initially welcoming IBM with open arms, now fear an IBM-dominated and controlled future. They are increasingly

(continued)

and desperately turning back to Apple as the only force that can ensure their future freedom.

IBM wants it all and is aiming its guns on its last obstacle to industry control: Apple. Will Big Blue dominate the entire computer industry, the entire information age? Was George Orwell right about 1984?

Jobs sets the stage with IBM as the villain and Apple as the hero; Apple is David to IBM's Goliath. Presenting the characters this way creates an emotional connection between the audience and Apple and evokes fear and suspicion of rival IBM.

The audience desires a final, climactic moment between the two parties. What will happen next?

The Suspense

When you tell a story, your goal is to keep your audience attentive, but keeping the audience's attention isn't just about being interesting. Make an unspoken promise to your audience that they will feel something at the end of your story. This will keep them intrigued, that an issue will be resolved or an idea will be revealed. The audience wants the answer, but not necessarily right away.

We crave wonder and mystery in stories, and as a presenter, you can build suspense by:

- *Giving the audience something to care about.* If the people in your audience care about what your hero is fighting for, they'll care about every challenge thrown your hero's way. Make sure the audience knows what can happen if the villain wins. The higher the stakes, the more your listeners will care.

- *Constantly challenging your hero.* The audience should never feel relaxed during your story. Keep throwing obstacles in your hero's path. This works best when your audience becomes emotionally invested in your hero's well-being. This will also demonstrate that your hero can handle adversity and continue to move forward for the benefit of the audience. Just make sure that challenges are not immediately resolved, as that can lose the audience's attention.

- *Identifying a story arc.* Maintain suspense by having the story unfold gradually. Follow a story arc. Here's a sample outline:
  - *Introduction:* Introduce the main character of the story.
  - *Conflict:* Introduce your villain and the conflict of the story.
  - *Rising action:* Describe the interactions between your hero and villain. They should challenge each other. It should be clear what happens if one or the other wins.
  - *Climax:* Focus on the biggest turning point for the hero, usually when he takes the biggest step outside his comfort zone.
  - *Falling action:* Approach the resolution.
  - *Resolution:* Reveal the final outcome. Is the hero or the villain the victor? Sometimes a resolution is not imminently clear if the audience is required to participate.

We use the Big Fish origin story in our pitches. To illustrate the story arc, see how we reveal and characterize a villain and hero and use suspense.

- *Introduction:* So why the name Big Fish Presentations? Well, four years ago, on a stormy night in January 2011, my cofounder, Gus Murillo, and I saw the most boring presentation of our lives. It was while attending a student organization meeting where a Fortune 500 executive blew us away with a presentation . . . but not in a good way.

- *Conflict:* I remember we were so excited to see this guy speak, but when he got up there, my eyes and ears were practically bleeding. It was 200 slides of nothing but text. I mean, c'mon, we've all seen this: the classic presenter who has big ideas but can't communicate them. To make matters worse, the guy answered his own questions, read off every single slide, and even laughed at his own jokes.

- *Rising action:* I thought to myself, "Presentations will never get much better." Then it hit me, "*Is this really the future of presentations?*" As I was sitting there for three hours, just lost, I had a crazy idea: What if there was a company that could not only offer great design but also help presenters better deliver their presentations? I felt that if the world's biggest companies are presenting like this, chances are, the next big idea won't be heard. If there was a company that could sync communication and design together, it would lead to more impactful presentations.

- *Climax:* That was when the idea for Big Fish Presentations was born.

- *Falling action:* Our purpose is nothing short of to help rid the world of boring presentations. Clients may be "small fish" with big ideas, but we'll help them present like "big fish" through our work. Gus and I decided to take a leap of faith and pursue this crazy idea.

- *Resolution:* Today we have helped companies of all sizes, from Fortune 100 companies to budding startups, deliver experiences to their audiences by combining presentation design, delivery, and video production. Working together, we can help you.

When it comes to storytelling, or presenting in general, your job is to keep the audience actively engaged.

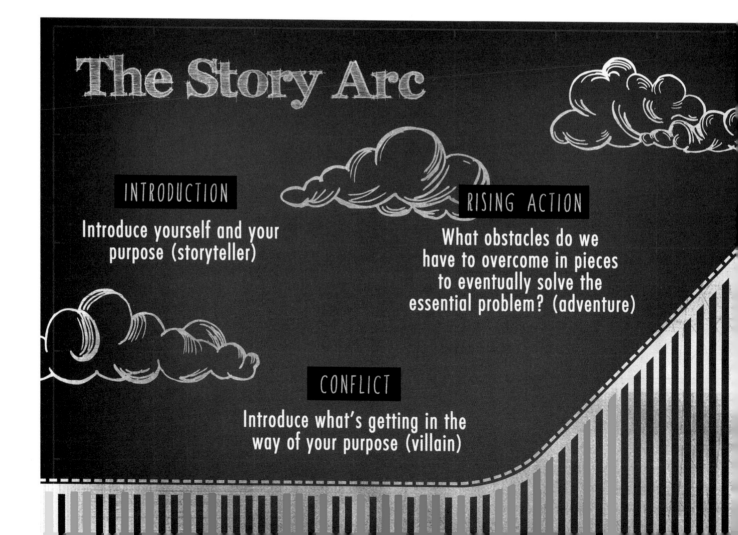

Building suspense is a game of momentum that takes the audience through a series of ups and downs. Your stories should invoke multiple emotions. However, keeping your listeners on their toes, minds racing, eyes wide, involves a certain level of interaction. To build suspense, you must avoid monotony by never being too consistent or staying in too much of a rhythm. You don't want to become predictable. Our eyes and ears are quick to pick up on patterns. This means that your audience will eventually identify your pattern, adjust to it, and glaze over the details or zone out.

———

At the heart of every great presentation is a well-crafted story. Using the three tenets of storytelling will help the audience relate to the content and context of your story, love the hero and hate the villain, and be riveted by the suspense. These all work together to help you persuade the audience of your ideas.

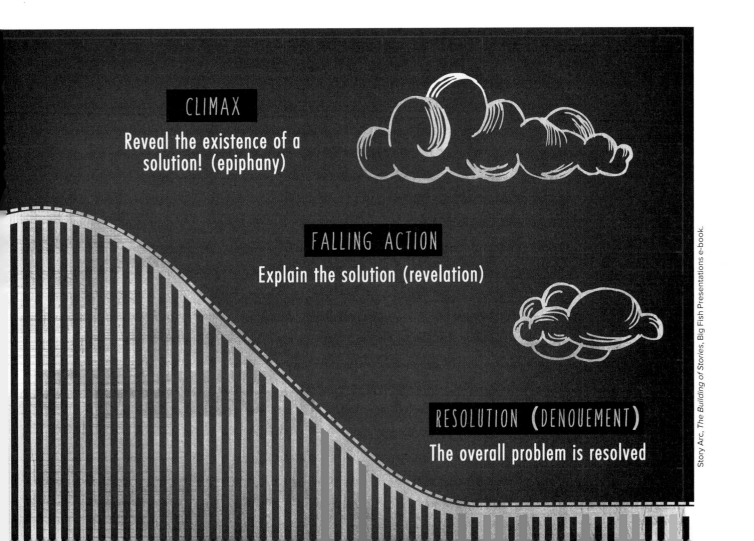

CLIMAX
Reveal the existence of a solution! (epiphany)

FALLING ACTION
Explain the solution (revelation)

RESOLUTION (DENOUEMENT)
The overall problem is resolved

Story Arc, *The Building of Stories*, Big Fish Presentations e-book.

DATA

In this chapter, we've talked a lot about building a narrative in your presentation. There is a story in everything, even data. Showing data doesn't have to be boring, monotonous, or confusing. You just have to use your imagination. We can tell you this book was written to represent our basic knowledge and understanding of presentations, or we can tell you this book is the hive mind of a group of individuals who've spent several years working on hundreds of presentations, putting thousands of hours into actual presentations that help illustrate the information in this book. Which one sounds better?

Make It Relevant

First things first: when presenting data, like everything else, it's important to make it relevant to the message and to your audience. Constantly reevaluate your content. Ask yourself, "Why would the audience care about this?" It is important for you to know the answer. You need to be able to explain to the audience why this data should be important to them. A great example is a popular press release issued by IBM in 2008 concerning the launch of its newest ultra-fast supercomputer, Roadrunner, which could perform 1,000 trillion calculations per second. How do you quantify that in terms that make sense to the average person? Remove the jargon that could alienate a portion of the audience and replace it with accessible and relatable language. The folks at IBM made this fact relevant by saying, "It would take the entire population of the earth—about six billion—each of us working a handheld calculator at the rate of one second per calculation, more than 46 years to do what Roadrunner

THEY'VE DONE STUDIES,
YOU KNOW. SIXTY PERCENT OF
THE TIME, IT WORKS EVERY TIME.

—BRIAN FANTANA,
Anchorman: The Legend of Ron Burgundy

can do in one day."[3] Amazing, right? While tech-savvy people might understand the initial statistic, this comparison makes the rest of us raise our eyebrows. If you can turn your high-level data into something people can relate to, individually or generally, then you fill a void with pure impact.

Kenny's Tip

Avoid jargon. Jargon that refers to industry-specific language can alienate others. And exile hackneyed phrases and buzzwords—"think outside the box," "cutting edge," and "innovative"—from your presentation. Using too much jargon can make you look like you're overcompensating for a lack of knowledge of your subject matter.

Hit 'Em in the Feels

If you want people to remember you and your message, you've got to make them feel something. For example, when Hans Rosling gave his TED talk, "The Best Stats You've Ever Seen," about the progress of global development, he slowly, and very passionately, dove into the facts, talked about what they meant to humankind as a whole, and created a sense of urgency for the audience. Rosling crafted a story that spans space and time with the oratory prowess of a seasoned preacher. He took the audience on a journey. He enabled them to understand the data so they could relate to it and be moved by it.

When incoporating data in your presentation, ask yourself:

- Who is my audience?

- Is the data relevant to my audience and my topic?

- Is the data presented in a simple and meaningful way?

- Can I get an emotional response by showing the data?

- What will my audience take away from this?

If you can answer all these questions accurately and confidently, then you are on your way to presenting data in a fun, interesting way. By the end of your talk, your audience will have a deeper understanding of the information you presented. Sometimes simply saying something isn't enough. Sometimes you need proof backed by solid data. If you can fix the normal disconnect that comes with relaying statistical and informative data, you can help the audience truly understand your message. Instead of people scratching their heads, trying to make sense of statistics and percentages, they will walk away with a bigger picture in mind—a picture you shared with them. Instead of numbers, they will see ideas. Instead of facts, they will have knowledge. Instead of watching a presentation, they will have been immersed in an experience.

Kenny's Tip

If you are presenting to a crowd that you are unfamiliar with and not all demographics can be known beforehand, ask yourself:

- Can I present the data in a way that makes people care?

- Can I show how the data affects their daily lives?

- Can I tell a simple story that explains their importance?

By answering these questions, you'll make it more likely that your data will speak to multiple demographics in the audience.

CALL TO ACTION

You need to know why you're doing what you're doing. A call to action is the reason you are presenting. Without a call to action, you have no purpose on stage. A good call to action should challenge listeners and make them feel like they've grown after they've accomplished it. The first thing you should do is figure out *why* you are presenting and how that challenges the audience's way of thinking.

This challenge is your call to action. The big idea and call to action go hand in hand. The big idea is the preview of your call to action. When building your content around a call to action, think of the following:

- What knowledge do the people in my audience possess prior to my call to action?

- What new information am I providing that will help them make a decision?

- What are the most important things the audience needs to know to make a decision?

- Have I successfully given my listeners all the resources they need to make a decision?

- What are the biggest obstacles that will prevent them from answering my call to action?

- What does my call to action bring to the audience?

You present a unique message, speak eloquently, transition well, and interact with the audience, supported by a gorgeous slide deck. However, none of this matters if you don't prompt your audience to take action in some way. After all, what is the goal of a presentation? We all present in order to create real, meaningful change. We want to influence people and make the world a better place. How do we do this? We have to instill within our listeners a sense of purpose. We have to impress a sense of urgency upon them. We have to create a call to action.

Throughout the presentation, you captivate people's eyes with design. You create a connection with your audience, intriguing them enough to listen to whatever it is you have to say. You tell them a story, transporting their minds and shifting their perspectives. You enthrall them with your message and move them enough to feel and think a certain way. However, without any direction, this is all in vain. The call to action points the user in a direction. You need to tell your audience what to do next. Over the course of your presentation, there are two places you can insert your call to action.

The first time you hint at it is during your thesis statement, where you can briefly address your purpose for speaking. You want to be up front about what you're trying to accomplish. If you're trying to raise money, begin by mentioning that you have an idea you believe in and that you hope to convince your audience of its merit by the end of your presentation. People will appreciate that you're being genuine, and they will be more willing to listen to you.

The second time you put forth a call to action is near the end of your presentation, after you make your last point but before you officially conclude. At this time, you can give a quick recap of your points, summarizing the most important topics you've discussed. Your supporting content will be the key to building credibility for your call to action. Once you have reminded your audience of what you've covered, you can tie in your call to action. This transition can be tricky. All of a sudden you are speaking directly to your audience, not just in hypotheticals. This is where you transform ideas into action.

You can do this in several ways:

- *The question,* or "big ask," requires your audience to think about what they are going to do about your topic. This is less demanding and lets people make their decision under little or no pressure. Instead of telling your listeners to do something, you are simply asking them to think. This way, you are providing them with an opportunity, but you are leaving the choice up to them, which empowers them.

   Example: "When are you going to do your part in the fight against world hunger?"

> *So go home tonight and ask yourselves, "What would I do if I weren't afraid?"*
>
> —SHERYL SANDBERG
> *COO of Facebook*

- *The demand* urges the audience to act immediately. This is more effective in situations where time is an issue. Remember, it's always better to be assertive than aggressive. You're not forcing the audience to do anything. Rather, you're presenting a scenario where the choice is obvious. From there, your built-up credibility can sway the audience to act on your recommendation.

  Example: "In this job market, either you brand yourself or you die."

- *The offer* immediately gives the audience something in return for action. People have a hard time turning down an easy deal, so by presenting them with a guaranteed prize of some kind, you are prompting action in your favor. This is for shorter sales in which you make the audience an "offer they can't refuse."

  Example: "If you sign up today, you will receive a free Visa gift card and a round-trip ticket to Sydney, Australia."

Remember, the more specific you are, the better. You don't want anything to be misconstrued. Be as direct as possible. If you want something, ask for it!

Creating and executing a call to action isn't easy. You don't want to come off as pushy, needy, or arrogant.

On the other hand, you don't want your presentation to be a waste of time. You need to accomplish something, but you can do it gracefully.

Our philosophy is based on the idea that you should always be as honest as possible with your audience. Being completely transparent can only improve your results after your call to action. One aspect of our philosophy stems from a well-known theory by inspirational speaker Simon Sinek. His "Start with Why" TED talk focuses on the idea that businesses should identify the "why" of their business before they think about how and what they do. Mediocre presentations only say what you do and how you do it. Identify all three, starting with "why," to build up your credibility, and then you can pull the trigger on that bold call to action. By answering the why, the what, and the how, rather than just the what, you create an emotional connection with your audience. Because people base their decisions more on emotion than on logic, your call to action will resonate more vibrantly.

Also, remember that it's OK to be creative in your call to action. In most cases, incorporating props, videos, images, or any other unique element into your presentation gives a tremendous boost to your likability. It signals the transition to the call to action, and it also makes the question, demand, or offer more obvious and memorable. Be different. Stand out. This is the time to put all your cards on the table, look people in the eye, and convince them that your cause or idea is worth supporting. It's your chance to convert your planning, practice, and performance into tangible results.

Make things happen.

Kenny's Tip

If you're working on your call to action last, your argument may not be as powerful. Your call to action should be the soul of your presentation, while the supporting content is its body.

My name is Maysoon Zayid, and if I can can, you can can.

—MAYSOON ZAYID
Comedian and Activist

Robin Marchant / Getty Images

STRUCTURE

When building your presentation, it's important to create a structure that allows your points to flow smoothly from one to another. If you move along too quickly, your audience might get lost or become confused. If you dwell on a topic for too long, your audience could get bored and zone out. If your structure isn't designed to grab interest quickly, transition smoothly, and close powerfully, the presentation will lose steam. This is why it's so important to preplan your presentation, at least to a certain extent. Structuring your presentation properly will help maintain the flow of your execution, the strength of your message, and the attention of your audience. Going into a presentation without any structure is like driving without a steering wheel: you have everything you need to move, but you have no control over where you're going. We don't want that to happen to you.

A good way to keep your mind focused and your audience hooked is to create a mental road map, which is an outline of your presentation prepared in advance that you can refer to as you go. Your road map comprises a strong opener, smooth transitions, and a powerful closer. Having this clear direction allows you to navigate easily through your presentation without rambling. It will also help you manage your time, which is absolutely crucial. If you don't devote the right amount of time to each section, you could miss or gloss over important points. Simulate the first few moments of being on stage. Choose the exact phrases you will use when you transition. Plan how you will wrap everything up.

Use the rule of threes to help the audience remember your key takeaways. If you can divide your content into three main points, your presentation will be exponentially more memorable. Obviously, there are some topics to which this rule doesn't apply, but it is very useful for most speeches. Before you share your main points, prime your audience with a statement like "In the next 25 minutes, you are going to learn three innovative ways to present better than you ever have." Saying something like this not only grabs your listeners' attention but also gives them a frame of reference for your presentation. As Dale Carnegie said, "Tell the audience what you're going to say, say it, then tell them what you've said." A bold opening statement primes the audience for your message, and a memorable closing

Kenny's Tip

Here's how to introduce the preview of topics. Do not say outright what the main points are. Don't ruin the surprise or suspense for the audience. Include the reward (what your listeners can gain by applying the main points). For example, "In *X* minutes (*X* being the estimated duration of the presentation), you will learn *Y* ways (*Y* being the number of main points) to *Z* (*Z* being your thesis statement or your preview of your call to action). This keeps your audience wanting more.

statement reaffirms it. This combination gives your words weight and causes your ideas to linger in people's minds during and after your presentation.

Here is a structure we recommend:

- *Introduction*
  - Opener (story, question, statistic, joke, quote, or attention grabber)
  - Explanation of opener (how does opener relate to theme of presentation?)
  - Preview of topics (provide the road map for the audience)
  - Thesis statement (preview of call to action)

- *Main points 1–3*
  - Body text that supports thesis statement
  - Transition statements that identify when moving from one main point to the next

- *Recap of topics.* Brief recap of main points and how they relate to call to action

- *Call to action*

- *Conclusion.* Closing (story, question, statistic, joke, quote, etc.—no new facts in conclusion)

You should elaborate on these, especially the main points. Working from a clear structure such as this will help you design your presentation. You can create slides that tell the audience where they are in the presentation and what to expect. Clear structure helps the audience as much as—or more than—it helps the presenter.

An excellent example of structure is the famous commencement speech given by Steve Jobs at Stanford. Jobs outlined his presentation by telling the audience he would relate three stories. After he delivered each story, he shared its message.

Another is the graduation address given by Admiral William H. McRaven at the University of Texas in 2014. In his speech, McRaven outlined 10 main points about how Navy SEAL training translates into success in life.

Both speakers gave the audience a preview of what was to come in their presentations.

We've talked about using a mental road map, managing the time for each section, using the rule of threes, and priming your audience. These are the factors that make up a structured presentation, but the ways in which you use them are entirely dependent on your personal style. Do what works best for you. In what order would you like to hear the information? How would you like the pacing, tone, and overall flow to feel—not as a presenter but as an audience member? Often we forget that the audience is made up of people just like us, which is why it's always good in presentation development to ask yourself, "Would I like this?"

Kenny's Tip

The element of suspense should apply not only to your stories but also to your entire presentation. Use the structure we provided in this section as the starting point for your content, design, and delivery.

Here are some ways to inject suspense into your presentation:

- *In content.* In your preview of topics, state, "In the next 45 minutes, you will learn three things to improve your life." You've primed the audience to watch for your three main points.

- *In design.* Putting only one idea on each slide prevents your listeners from getting ahead of you. It keeps them actively engaged as you reveal each idea.

- *In delivery.* Right before you deliver a point, pause. If done properly, this will create instant tension.

LINES THAT STICK

Being memorable is about standing out for a specific and powerful reason. It's about being unique, having an impact. By using powerful language, you have the ability to communicate ideas that may stand the test of time. Years after your presentation, your words may still be quoted.

We remember certain words and phrases because they mean something to us. So in order to be memorable, you need to provide meaning. You have to craft your words in a way that makes the audience not just think but feel something. You have to find the heart of the idea before you can hope for it to be meaningful and therefore memorable. The most impactful quotes are the ones that speak about a big idea, but in a short, direct way. You'll want to keep this in mind as you write your own presentation.

Carmine Gallo, bestselling author of *Presentation Secrets of Steve Jobs*, says that a good rule of thumb for writing memorable lines is to keep them down to 140 characters or less. This way your message can be short, memorable, and easily shared. Think of your big line as something you would like to see and share on Twitter or Facebook.

Another way to think about this is through slogans or taglines. Think of your favorite brands. For instance, what computer do you own? Is there a specific company you purchase your shoes, shirts, or food from? Take Disneyland as an example. Its slogan is "The happiest place on earth." Disneyland distilled its purpose into a single phrase.

Here are some of our favorite memorable lines:

Be the change you want to see in the world.
—MAHATMA GANDHI

*Our books and our pens are
the most powerful weapons.*
—MALALA YOUSAFZAI

*Everyone you will ever meet knows
something you don't.*
—BILL NYE

*Your education is a dress rehearsal for
a life that is yours to lead.*
—NORA EPHRON

*If you want to change the world,
start off by making your bed.*
—ADMIRAL WILLIAM H. MCRAVEN

(Continued)

Quotes like these are very memorable because they say a lot using very few words. The key is simplifying a complex idea. This doesn't mean your entire presentation should hinge on a few words, but it does mean that a few words can make your entire presentation more memorable. You want your presentation to be talked about, shared, and used as a reference or guide.

You want it to be easily translatable or transferable. You want the takeaway to be simple and bold. You want to craft something that can be explained in a sentence but talked about for years.

So how do you create these magical lines? The best way to write a good line is to make sure the rest of your

Gandhi, Omikron Omikron/Science Source/Getty Images; Bill Nye, NASA/GSFC/Bill Hrybyk; Admiral William H. McRaven from the U.S. Navy Biography Website;

Malala Yousafzai, JStone/Shutterstock.com; Nora Ephron, s_bukley/Shutterstock.com.

Your calling isn't something that somebody can tell you about. . . . You know it inside yourself.
—OPRAH WINFREY

If you're going through hell, keep going.
—WINSTON CHURCHILL

Never doubt that a small group of thoughtful, committed citizens can change the world. Indeed, it is the only thing that ever has.
—MARGARET MEAD

When fate hands you a lemon, make lemonade.
—DALE CARNEGIE

Here's the tricky thing about language: it lies about how powerful it is.
—LENA DUNHAM

presentation is completely finished. Once you have established everything you want to say, then you can delve into the single most important aspect of your presentation. For instance, when Steve Jobs said, "Today Apple reinvents the phone!" he already knew the structure of his presentation. He covered the three aspects of the iPhone before he even made this statement. He knew that this would be the big announcement, the kernel of truth that everyone was going to remember. He could have picked a line about the marriage of music and communication. After all, Apple was known for its iPod at the time. Instead, he chose to

Winston Churchill from the Imperial War Museums Collection; Dale Carnegie, Alfred Eisenstaedt/The LIFE Picture Collection/Getty Images; Oprah Winfrey, Jaguar PS/Shutterstock.com; Margaret Mead, Photo Collection Anefo of Nationaal Archief; Lena Dunham, Jaguar PS/Shutterstock.com.

Kenny's Tip

I find that the best times to use lines are when I am making my thesis statement, introducing an idea, explaining a complex topic, or closing my presentations.

make a bolder statement. He claimed that he had re-invented the telephone. It was a huge deal. It made an impact. We still remember it.

To find your own lines, all you have to do is decide what is most important in your presentation. You know your content, and you can deliver it well, but can you boil it down to something people will be able to carry with them? Can you infuse your words with passion and confidence? Anyone can give a presentation, but not everyone can leave behind a timeless statement. If an idea is meaningful, the message marketable, and your words memorable, you can truly change the world.

STEVE JOBS

MacWorld Expo 2007

David Paul Morris/
Getty Images News/Getty Images

MAKE ANYTHING INTERESTING

There's an unfair assumption about presentations in general: they're boring. Don't believe us? Get on Twitter. Type "presentations" into the search bar. Switch the results from "top" to "recent." More than likely, you'll see two narratives when it comes to presentations: "I have so much anxiety" or "This is going to be so boring." When it comes down to it, yes, some presentations are boring—it has absolutely nothing to do with the topic.

Famous ad man George Lois once claimed he could sell anything. He said he could sell you a pen by making you understand it was the best pen in the world. It was the pen you needed. It was *the* pen. Through him, it became the pen you wanted. This is relevant, because it conveys a message: *there's no such thing as a boring topic.*[4]

If George Lois can make a living from selling pens, then you can make your audience care about your message. You don't have to make the topic interesting; you have to make the way you present it interesting.

How?

Be Yourself

Many get caught up in how they should behave when presenting.

Don't be rigid or sterile. Be casual. Be entertaining and fun. If the topic isn't necessarily the most exciting thing, acknowledge it and overdeliver! (If you believe your topic is boring, it may be time to reevaluate what the topic means to you and what it should mean

If people like you, they'll listen to anything you have to say.

—GARY VAYNERCHUK
Social Marketing Expert

HubSpot INBOUND and Gary Vaynerchuk

to your audience.) Don't separate yourself from the people in your audience by thinking there's some mysterious fourth wall between them and you. If you're relaxed, confident, and genuine, your vibe will be contagious.

Here are some ways to make any topic interesting:

- *After figuring out your big idea, create a headline that gives the audience a preview of your talk.* A good headline has some shock value that creates intrigue and expectation. The title "2015 Data Report" is boring, so why not change it to "Going from $500,000 to $1 Million: How We Grew 100% in 2015"? TED talks are great examples of good presentation titles that are either intriguing or downright controversial. A few standouts:
  - What I Learned as a Kid in Jail (Ismael Nazario)
  - How I Held My Breath for 17 Minutes (David Blaine)
  - 10 Things You Didn't Know About an Orgasm (Mary Roach)
  - The Price of Shame (Monica Lewinsky)
  - I Got 99 Problems . . . Palsy Is Just One (Maysoon Zayid)

- *Engage with the audience.* By asking the members of your audience how much they know about the subject you're presenting, you instantly gain their attention and participation. Whether it's through a live poll or by asking your listeners to tweet you questions, you connect with them and get them to engage more deeply with your content. Just make sure your content is relevant to the audience.

- *Go analog.* If your topic is very complex, but you feel like you can explain it more simply without a slide show, go ahead. This will let the audience focus on you.

- *Focus on your body language.* It's important that you appear excited about your content when you present. Your body language is key to making the audience believe, listen, and trust you. After all, if you're not excited about your subject, why should the audience be?

- *Take complex lines and make them simple yet memorable.* If you have complex data, deliver it in short, memorable lines.

- *Use humor and storytelling to make dense, yet critical, topics interesting.* When presenting data, make sure the audience knows how it relates to and affects their daily lives.

It's important to understand that the audience isn't a vicious group of critics. Remember that they are just like you. They eat; they sleep; they feel emotions; they put their pants on one leg at a time; and they all want to be entertained. By being yourself, you let your audience know you're human. By getting in the mindset that the people in the crowd aren't there to judge you, but rather to hear what you have to say, you understand that they're human, too. It's with this realization that you enable yourself to share something they aren't expecting: your personality.

Become the Audience

To become the crowd, you need to understand exactly what your listeners need from your topic. Imagine if George Lois asked you to present that pen he wants to sell. There's nothing special about it. It's just a pen. However, you can't tell the audience that. Remember: You have to make people want that pen, because nobody is sitting in his or her chair waiting for it. It's not about the pen; it's about what someone can do with it.

Focus on the audience's wants—the benefits your topic brings to a specific need. If you're presenting to a group of teachers about a new copier, don't talk about the technical aspects of the copier, such as how the processing chip allows for more copies in less time. Talk about how much time the teachers are going to save because the copier is so much faster; and less time copying tests means more time for other things, such as family.

See where this is going? Sell the sizzle, not the steak.

CONCLUSION

What you say is important, but how you say it is more important.

Your audience is composed of many people, all with varied points of view. Their minds work in different ways. Once you understand how they like to hear information and what interests them, you can captivate them in a way that no one else can. It is an extremely valuable skill to be able to open your presentation, convey data, and leave your listeners with a feeling or impulse that inspires them to do something.

Content is just the beginning. If content is king, then design is its queen.

Challenges

NOVICE

- Create a presentation using the Big Fish Presentations structure (opener, preview of topics, big idea, main points, recap, call to action, conclusion).

- Tell a story with a hero, villain, and suspense that is related to the topic of your presentation.

- Use the rule of three in identifying your main points.

EXPERT

- When citing a statistic, show how it relates directly to the audience and why it should matter to them.

- Distill the big idea of your presentation into a "tweetable line" (140 characters or less).

- Prime the audience with a road map of your presentation.

DESIGN

> *The aim of art is to represent not the outward appearance of things, but their inward significance.*
>
> —ARISTOTLE

Your idea might sound great on paper, but can it move past the page?

As a presenter, your goal is to create change. You want to change worldviews, habits, mindsets, and sometimes just your audience's morning routine. But your goal is to have people walk in one way and walk out another. Otherwise, you did not make the difference that you set out to make. When you weigh all the tools at your disposal as a presenter, you need to consider one of the most powerful: design.

As noted earlier, if content is king, then design is its queen. But why does making something look nice even matter?

Never discount the power of good design. Design is like art, and art is powerful: it can make you laugh, it can make you cry, and it can make you question everything around you. Like art, design can be used to make a difference in the world.

In this chapter, we'll discuss the following:

- STRUCTURE YOUR SLIDE DECK
- NOTE FROM KENNY: FROM CONTENT TO DESIGN
- STORYBOARDING
- WHAT MAKES A GOOD SLIDE?
- COLOR
- VISUAL HIERARCHY
- TYPOGRAPHY
- ARTWORK
- MOTION
- DATA
- HANDOUTS
- TOOLS BEYOND POWERPOINT
- TIME CRUNCH

STRUCTURE YOUR SLIDE DECK

What Goes in Your Deck?

You have crafted your big idea and central message. What should go in your deck? This simple question seems to be one that many presenters struggle with. It is often a case of too much information packed on each slide, too many slides, or both. The horrible presentation that sparked the creation of Big Fish had this as a major issue. The presenter did not know what to put on the slides, so he included everything, even if it was super boring and irrelevant. Let's not do that when creating our presentations.

How do you decide what becomes a slide?

SCRIPT

Before working on your slides, you need to know what you are going to say. Work on your script and create a high-level outline of what you want to include. We see a lot of scripts that are convoluted and too detailed. People sacrifice stories for data and end up overloading their audiences. A high-level outline will enable you to identify the information that supports your main points. If any information doesn't fall within the outline, leave it out. This will help you be concise. The audience doesn't want to hear about every aspect of your product or every detail of your story. You want to give a clear and concise message that describes your big idea and supports your central message. Anything tangential should be left out.

Whether you are telling a story, outlining a process, or proposing a new idea, your presentation should have structure. The first slides should contain your main takeaways, simple concise messages for better audience comprehension and recall. These are the backbone of your presentation.

This will help you organize all supporting information under these sections. As a presenter, your information has to be intentional. When you lay out these major points, you now have a framework for what deserves to go in your deck. Most or all of your talk will fall under your main points and will be easier for your audience to remember if broken down into distinct sections.

You have your main points. Now consider which of your supporting or secondary information deserves to go on a slide. Consider your main takeaways and then decide what information will best reinforce the key messages. If you are making an argument for a new idea or concept, your best supporting information will be the proof points that are the most convincing and crucial. If you are selling a product, your best supporting information will be the major benefits that will appeal to clients. If you are telling a compelling story about your struggle through adversity, your supporting information will be the highlights of the events that took place and got you where you are today. If you have information that doesn't fall under any of your main points, consider if this reinforces your central message before including it blindly in your presentation.

What Goes on a Slide?

There is no prescribed formula to determine what information should be on a slide for every presentation situation. The most important thing to remember is to ensure that each slide has a purpose. You may have an idea for a slide that might "look beautiful," but you must consider if this actually supports the overall message of the presentation.

An ideal slide contains only one idea that captures the audience's attention. It provides absolute focus.

How do you reduce clutter on a slide? Focus on two things: what the audience is seeing on the slide and what the audience is hearing from you.

Let's say you have a slide full of text. Nobody is going to read all that, and if you think anyone is going to remember it, you're insane. First, you need to limit yourself: make sure no slide has more than three sentences. Even three is pushing it, but we're being generous. In those three sentences, make sure none is longer than 15 words. A sentence with only 15 words is appealing to readers and will force you to be brief.

Too Much Clutter

- Decreasing the amount of clutter you have in your script and on your slides is important.
- No one wants to read a ton of information on a slide. This takes attention away from you, the speaker.
- Are you still reading this? That's incredible. Feel free to stop.
- See how distracting this is?

REDUCE CLUTTER

Set yourself apart by decreasing the amount of text on your slides.

Think about it. Would you rather see seven bullet points or two?

What sentence is more appealing to you, the question we've conveniently put in its own paragraph above or the over-15-word run-on this sentence is turning out to be?

Remember, you should have only one idea or one message per slide. Each slide needs to stand on its own. It should not be dependent on any other slide to justify or explain its meaning. If you put more than one idea on a slide, you risk distracting your audience.

We know what some of you are thinking right now: "But I have all these regulations, stipulations, and important policies that the audience needs to see." No, the audience doesn't. If what you're showing is really *that* important, putting it on a slide that will be on a screen for maybe five minutes is a horrible idea. This is not a good way to foster audience comprehension and retention. You can give people a handout, direct them to a microsite, or pick three of the most important parts, but please don't put the 25 tenets of your company on one slide and expect everyone to remember them.

How do you stick to one idea per slide? Let's put this into practice: If I'm thinking of creating a slide that says "Hiring Great Salespeople," with three supporting bullet points below, I could put each bullet point on its own slide. This will enable me to focus people's attention on each point rather than having them see and think about all the points at once. If you are worried about the audience not being able to follow along, then include a small reminder of the section somewhere on the slide so they know what the overarching idea is.

Kenny's Tip

If you are presenting to a technical and analytical bunch (we're looking at our friends in pharmaceuticals, biology, and engineering), a lot of information needs to be conveyed (sometimes for legal reasons). If you must include certain pieces of information in your presentation, my recommendation is to reduce the clutter on the slide in the formal presentation (rehearse your information well) and provide the audience with a comprehensive handout, digital PDF, website, or blog reference with more details about what you discussed. Apple is the poster child of this practice. All the tech details can be found on the website after a product announcement. During an Apple presentation of a new product, the audience sees visuals of the specs as they are discussed.

What do you do when you have a list of points that support an idea? Show the list visually by using icons or photos instead of a bunch of crowded bullets.

We know these tips aren't fun or easy to follow, but you'll thank us when your presentation is devoid of all the dead weight. While there's no cure-all solution to clutter, these restrictions will force you to get rid of all the extraneous material.

We showed you how to reduce what the audience is seeing. Keep in mind that the slides should not distract the audience from your words and vice versa. Make sure the slides complement your presentation or at least guide it.

How Do You Determine Slide Deck Length?

What constitutes too many or too few slides?

There is no single answer to this question. As we craft the stories and presentations for clients and ourselves, we consider all the factors surrounding the talk and ask the following questions:

- *How strong a presenter am I?* Am I carrying the presentation, or is it a slide show?

- *How long is my talk?* Do I have a time limit, or is it up to me?

- *Who are my listeners?* Will they need a simple concise message in less than 10 slides because their time and attention are limited?

- *What am I trying to say?* What style will best reinforce the message that I am trying to get across? Do I need a lot of slides to show data trends? Or do I need just three or four slides to show who I am and what I stand for?

Asking yourself these questions will help you determine the right number of slides. And sometimes the answer is no slides at all. While what goes in the deck is important, we firmly believe that you should be able to deliver your presentation without a deck. On the other end of the spectrum, we also understand that a high slide count could be beneficial to bring the audience through the information. Just remember, the more slides, the more pressure on the presenter. You will need to make sure that you are timing your slides well.

Let's look at an example.

CASE STUDY

At the Apple event in September 2013, Apple SVP of worldwide marketing, Phil Schiller, introduced two new phones to the world at once; this is the first time Apple had ever done this. In Phil's 10-minute introduction to the iPhone 5c, he used 30 slides and 2 videos for his talk. In the roughly six minutes that he spoke, he used about five slides a minute. This is more on the fast-paced end for slides, but his relatively high slide count makes sense for the context of his talk. Phil Schiller is a strong speaker and felt comfortable moving through the slides at a quick pace. He had only six minutes to show a brand-new product loaded with many features, so he moved through the information with brevity but not with haste.

The audience consisted of a wide variety of consumers, reporters, and tech geeks who understand and appreciate innovation as well as emerging tech trends. This group can absorb small, digestible snippets of information within a larger number of slides; these people were most likely to digest the most information about the 5c in the shortest period of time. Apple has consistently been acknowledged for its level of presentation simplicity and skill, and this is evident throughout this entire keynote (which can be viewed at http://www.apple.com/apple-events /september-2013/).[1]

This is just one example of how slide count is highly dependent on the context of the talk. Consider all your available options and choose one that will best suit you as a presenter. Don't feel bad if you don't make the right choice at first. Experiment. Occasionally step out of your comfort zone and try something new. You may find that the new style works better for you.

PHIL SCHILLER

Apple Product Launch, September 10, 2013

Justin Sullivan/Getty Images

NOTE FROM KENNY: FROM CONTENT TO DESIGN

In the beginning of my career, I performed many rapid-fire presentations successfully with 75 to 100 slides. It wasn't until recently that I switched to using fewer slides or none at all when giving my talks. I found that fewer slides pose fewer distractions for the audience. Here's a story from my actual notes on an event.

I was returning as the opening speaker at a large conference and was asked to do something different from my usual shtick on presentations. I was asked to speak about my other passion: entrepreneurship. I did not have a slide deck on this subject prepared. Big Fish was slammed with work, and the members of my own team told me they couldn't do anything for me except touch things up (that's tough love for you!). Seeing as I was on my own for this one, I promptly got to work.

First, I came up with the big idea: "If you want your business not only to survive but to thrive in this economic environment, you will need constantly to refine your three Ps of organizational success: people, passion, process."

From this big idea, I built a content structure based on the Big Fish outline process. (Note: Don't be intimidated by the length of this outline. It's not as scary as it seems. In Chapter 4, "Delivery," we'll explain how rehearsing the presentation in parts *before* actually delivering the presentation as a whole assists in retention. I put a lot of emphasis on the closer.)

Use your outline to identify what needs to go on a slide and what doesn't.

Writing an outline involves five things:

1. <u>Underline</u> content that can be easily represented on a slide as a main point and also be visually represented in a powerful way.

2. **Boldface** anything intended to be powerful and emphasized, such as an easy-to-tweet line that requires a pause upon delivery.

3. *Italicize* lines that introduce the big idea.

4. Use bullet points in the outline to move the presentation forward (no fluff).

5. Use **<u>boldface and underlining</u>** to represent the performance of a specific delivery gesture or physical act.

For this presentation, I had two standing whiteboards on opposite sides of the stage.

Here is an outline of the speech:

SOFT OPENER

- Ask how many people have attended this conference before.

- Tell the audience not to be afraid of interacting with each other. <u>[Use a black slide for first slide, to build suspense.]</u>

OPENER

- Tell the story of Big Fish Presentations in January 2010 and progress made by January 2012. <u>[Introduce logo of Big Fish after telling story.]</u>

- From running a business while in school, a problem arose: **What did I want to do with my life?**

- Problem arose due to common issue with schools: **School never taught me to follow my passion. School always taught me how to get a job.**

- Schools normally taught this process: <u>Studying Hard + Working Hard + High-Paying Job = Happiness.</u> [Show slide of points laid out like an equation.]

- Dropped out of school after hearing Dad tell a story. More on that later.

- Fast-forward to 2014. Big Fish has worked with some of the largest brands in the world. Currently working on first book to be published by McGraw-Hill.

- *Write this down: People + Passion + Process = Profit. I'm going to share with you how you can take this formula and apply it to make your business not only survive but also thrive in this tough economic environment.* <u>[Introduce title slide: "Three Ps of Organizational Success."]</u>

- If you don't have a business now, listen anyway. You will still learn the secrets to help your future business grow.

- State transition to main point 1: *people.*

MAIN POINT 1: PEOPLE [slide with photo of people of Big Fish and the word "People" on it]

- **Great organizations need great people.**

- Not every organization is a fit with the employee.

- Show funny video from Valentine's Day [to see this video, check out our YouTube page: youtube.com /bigfishpresentations].

- It's important to hire people who are a right fit for the job, both technically and culturally.

- **We hire our best employees using the following methods:** [Show slides with main points individually to build up importance and speak more about each.]

  1. Referral from a trusted employee.

  2. Gut feeling. If I can acknowledge this person is coachable, is likable, and has a minimum level of expertise that's acceptable, that's a good sign.

  3. A clever cover letter that shows the candidate's personality:

     a. Check out this cover letter from Rob, our copywriter. [Show cover letter from Rob. Highlight sentences to refer to points previously stated. This is a hilarious letter. If we get enough requests, we may be willing to share it with everyone.]

     b. We knew we wanted to hire Rob because his letter was sincere, passionate, and honest.

- **People buy from people.** Having the right team can help you foster relationships with potential clients.

- Tell story of acquisition of recent largest client due to customer service and company culture.

- **Your team is the company's greatest asset.**

- State transition to main point 2: *passion*.

MAIN POINT 2: PASSION [slide with photo of heart and the word "Passion" on it]

- **The best way to showcase passion is to be so good at what you do that people can't ignore you.**

- Tell first Raising Cane's pitch story. [Show slide of Raising Cane's logo or chicken fingers.]

- Say line: "We're going to trust a 20-year-old with the CEO's presentation?"

- Paraphrase response: "I may be 20, but I promise you no one will work harder to make a great presentation. I will do whatever it takes, and if you are not satisfied, I'll gladly refund you the money."

- Raising Cane's works with us regularly.

- Great people and great company to work with.

- The company understands the content of this presentation very well.

- **If you're passionate about something, be the best at it that you can be and share that passion with the world.**

- In anything, being so good that people have to notice you is the way to success and fulfillment.

- **If you're not comfortable with what you're doing, you've just wasted seconds, minutes, hours, and days you'll never get back.**

- State transition to main point 3: *process*.

MAIN POINT 3: PROCESS [slide with photo of a gear and word "Process" on it]

- Record everything to repeat success and to prevent failure. [Show slide of excerpts from *Big Fish Sales + Account Management* manual.]

- Creating processes has allowed us to: [Show slides with main points individually to build up importance; speak more about each.]

    1. Measure success and failure more accurately

    2. Maintain consistency

    3. Help train new people

    4. Scale as needed

    5. Keep a standard

- Ultimate goal in documenting processes: **make excellence and growth a habit.**

- State transition to recap of points.

RECAP OF POINTS [slide with "The Three Ps of Organizational Success"]

- As business grows, nothing will become more valuable than: [Show photos of each main point individually to build up importance.]

    1. The people you employ

    2. The processes you have in place to grow

    3. Your passion to fight through the tough times:

        a. These three elements are important to grow a profit in your business.

        b. Don't do it only for a profit.

        c. The best businesses build the entrepreneur financially and personally.

- Transition to closing/call to action with story from Dad: **"As we end our journey, here's the story from my father I promised to share."**

- "I truly believe it reflects the spirit of every entrepreneur."

CLOSING/CALL TO ACTION [slide with picture of Dad and friends]

- Tell story of "point A to point B" from Dad.

- **<u>Draw point A on whiteboard 1 and point B on whiteboard 2. Do hand gesture of straight line between two boards.</u>**

- His friend didn't want to do it for himself; he wanted to do it for the status.

- Dad did it differently. **Do it not for the money but for the fulfillment.**

- Dad's response: "While your path may be a straight line from point A to point B, my path will be different, but the ending will be the same. My path will be filled with lines, curves, and eraser marks but will end up at point B. The difference is that in those lines, curves, and erasures, I will experience more life than you ever would because I am doing what I love." [Paraphrase.]

- <u>**Do a hand gesture of a squiggly line between whiteboards. [I promise this was way cooler in execution than on paper.]**</u>

- Share where Dad is today.

- **This is the story my father told me when I needed encouragement to follow my passion and asked him for guidance.**

- This story helped me, and I hope it helps you follow your passion.

- Life's going to give you crazy turns, erasures, and scratches.

- **When it does, step back and remind yourself why you're going to point B in the first place. That's what I ask of you. *Do not give up*. [Call to action.]**

- **Don't be just out to make a buck; make your dent in the universe.**

- **Be the best version of you that you can be.**

- **By being you, you will forever be an original and never, ever die a copy.**

- **And that in itself is worth more than anything you can put in a bank.**

- <u>Thank you. [Show animated logo at the end.]</u>

This presentation led to the formula I use for my keynote slides now:

- Black slide

- Photograph relevant to opener (my opener + explanation of opener)

- Title screen (usually animated motion graphic)

- The big idea (thesis statement)

- Main point 1

- Supporting content for main point 1 (usually a photograph or video)

- Main point 2

- Supporting content for main point 2 (usually a photograph or video)

- Main point 3

- Supporting content for main point 3 (usually a photograph or video)

- Recap of main points

- Call to action

- Conclusion

- Ending title slide (usually animated motion graphic)

You may use this outline for your presentations. Add slides to this deck that you deem important.

If you have more complex slides that will not emotionally resonate with the audience, hook them in the opener with emotionally driven material. If you do use heavy data in the beginning, make sure to explain *why* the data is important to the audience. (For example, "Based on this chart, we hit quarter 1 financial projections" is not enough. Instead, "Based on this chart, we hit quarter 1 financial projections, *which means raises for everyone*.")

Create and choose the slides that enhance your presentation and deliver an experience to the audience.

STORYBOARDING

What Is Storyboarding?

You've heard the term before. For writers and directors in the movie industry, a "storyboard" helps visualize how a script on the page will look as scenes on the screen. The storyboard is an essential part of the storytelling process.

This is where a story is tested. "A lot of things come to light that aren't clear when you are just reading words on a page."[2] You start to see some of the holes or the need to change wording or order to make the movie cohere. Storyboards allow the director to map out each scene visually as he or she plans for production.

How does this translate to presentations? If you have decided that you will be using a slide deck, a storyboard can help you plan the visual presentation. It will help you to design each slide and to realize what works and won't work for your visual story. It also saves time. If you've sketched out your entire slide deck on a storyboard, you can make changes, delete, or reorganize it until you are happy with it before you actually begin creating the slides. Slide creation will be that much easier. A storyboard is the visual equivalent of an outline for your talk. Don't worry about the specifics of the design; focus instead on the visual concepts.

How does this actually work? Let's look at a few ways it's done.

One way is to draw your slides by hand. You can use sticky notes (one note with one idea per slide) that you can move around on a wall.[3] Or you can lay them out in a notebook or on sheets of paper.

Kenny's Tip

On the bottom of each sticky note, I like to add notes about the most important things I need to say on that slide. If there are too many important things, I distribute the content among different slides.

You can also put your ideas on a whiteboard. At the Big Fish offices, most designers are given a glass desk on which they can storyboard their presentations with dry-erase markers. Storyboarding your slides on a whiteboard is also helpful because it's easy to change. If your visuals don't work, erase them and start again. This is also good for working in groups. Putting everything on a whiteboard for everyone to tear apart or build on allows for a collaborative storyboarding process.

Tech Platforms

There are a variety of online and offline platforms that you can use in planning your visuals. The "slide sorter view" in PowerPoint enables you to sketch out your presentation.[4]

Prezi is a presentation platform that also works well for storyboarding your presentation. It is presentation software that allows a team to storyboard together from various locations. You're able to build your storyboard in a nonlinear fashion, similar to what you would do on a whiteboard, but on the web.

It enables you to save and share your ideas easily within a group. However, it does come with a learning curve and is sometimes more time-consuming than using sticky notes or a whiteboard.

How to Storyboard

Take your script or the copy you have planned for each slide and begin thinking of visual ways to display the information. This is visual brainstorming. Don't be afraid. All ideas are welcome, and sometimes the craziest ideas are the ones that make the most impact. Take the time to think of a few different visual concepts for each slide, and then decide which will make the most impact. Here is a simple process that you can follow when you consider what visuals to use on which slide.

Evaluate

You created the content and know it like the back of your hand, but you need to consider what it means for the audience. Let's take this statement: "Forty million dollars of capital investments raised to aid in sustainable growth." What are you trying to convey?

What is the main takeaway? Option 1: We want to emphasize the amount of capital investment. Option 2: We want to show that we are trying to build for sustainable growth. Forty million dollars is important, but it's not the most important piece of information.

Ideate

Now that you know what you want to say, how can you show this in a way that will reinforce your main takeaway?

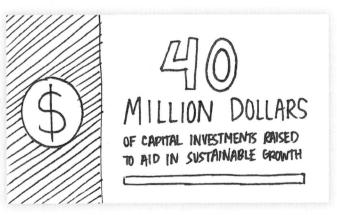

OPTION 1

40 MILLION DOLLARS OF CAPITAL INVESTMENTS RAISED — TO AID IN — SUSTAINABLE GROWTH

OPTION 2

This three-step process will become second nature as you go through it. You are working on the aesthetics of your message. This means you need to consider not only the actual design but also the effect it will have on people. The harder and smarter you work on your visuals, the more they will help you make an impact.

Refine

Scrap the visual concepts that don't reinforce your message. Take a step back and examine your slide. If it takes more than a second or two to determine the core meaning, then you've got some work to do. Use trial and error to trim the fat from your presentation. Keep it interesting, but keep it clean. Once you have filtered out the unnecessary elements, you can proceed with your design.

Kenny's Tip

A good rule of storyboarding is to ask, "So what?" about each slide. While design is great, it's important to ask: "Is this slide significant in the development of the presentation? Does it have compelling content?" Never pad your deck with unnecessary slides.

WHAT MAKES A GOOD SLIDE?

Slides have many different contexts; there are slides that are presented, e-mailed, or viewed on the web. They all serve different purposes (and because of this, there are characteristics that may be good in some contexts and bad in others). Some are meant to highlight the most important points of a speaker's presentation, as visual guideposts on a journey the audience is taking. Others are meant to be consumed online, absent a speaker, and must contain more comprehensive information.

We have seen enough slides in our experience, from bad to great, to determine the characteristics that all great slides have in common. Here are case studies of three of the most important ones, illustrated with work we have done for our clients.

Kenny's Tip

When I see a good slide, I feel that the text complements the presenter, not overwhelms him or her. Type, graphics, and overall art appeal are important, but if the slide is overloaded with information, then you have a handout on the screen, not a presentation. I want to be able to follow the presenter rather than know what the presenter is about to say. That is one of the surest ways to boredom.

SIMPLE

Simple slides utilize digestible bits of information that captivate people's attention and enhance understanding and recall while keeping them invested in what you are saying. Do not overload the audience. Overload doesn't refer just to text. It applies to graphics, photos, animation—anything that can bombard your audience with too much information.

We've helped many healthcare companies tell their information-filled stories in a simple way. For our client *Palleck Orthodontics*, we designed clutter-free slides with minimal text that helped the audience focus on the presenter—not the slide.

CASE STUDY

UNDERSTANDABLE

The goal is to engage, not distract. Merely "pretty" slides don't serve a purpose. A slide must have meaning, and the audience must easily understand that meaning.

How do you make difficult financial concepts understandable and relatable? For Big Fish client *Wheelhouse Analytics*, we replaced bland charts, graphs, and definitions with a clear flowchart to help financial advisors grasp the content on each slide quickly and easily.

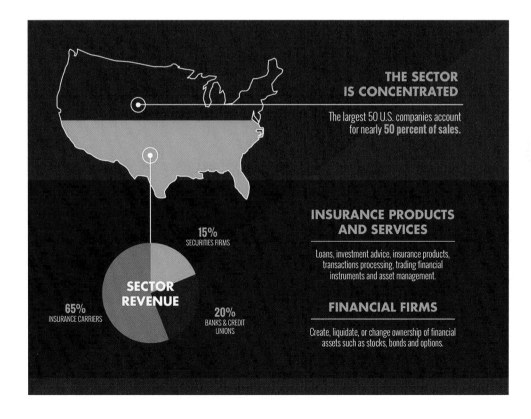

CASE STUDY

MEMORABLE

Slides that are beautiful and evoke emotion help the audience remember your message. When you see a presentation with the exact same template and layout for every slide, do you remember it? No. Does seeing the company logo on every slide help you remember the company? No. This is why we consider color, visual hierarchy, typography, animation, and data visualization. These elements help people engage with and recall your content, which may influence them to make the desired change.

When you hear about a startup that creates reading glasses, it doesn't really sound like a company you would remember. But what about a company that brings affordable eyewear to less-developed areas across the world and has a measurable economic impact?

For inspirational startup *Harambee*, we intentionally designed the first slide to appear fuzzy and out of focus. The audience would see that there was text on the slide but would find it hard to read. On the next slide, we removed the fuzzy layer, revealing the text in sharp focus. We re-created for the audience the difference a pair of reading glasses could make on the lives of those who need them.

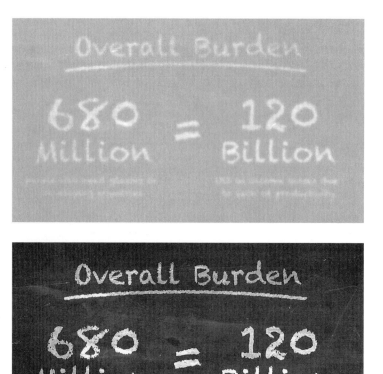

color interactions are complementary colors and analogous colors. Complementary colors are colors that lie on opposite sides of the color wheel. Analogous colors lie next to each other on the color wheel. Choosing a scheme that makes good use of one of these types of interactions will ensure that your colors do not clash with each other.

Another factor to consider when deciding color is the presentation platform you're using. Most presentations are designed in programs such as Microsoft PowerPoint, Apple Keynote, and Prezi. These programs are digitally based, and many work best in an RGB (red, green, and blue) format. RGB is used for any design displayed digitally, while CMYK (cyan, magenta, yellow, and black) is used in print. You will see RGB options in many of these programs that allow you to adjust the red, green, and blue components of the colors you are using to get to a specific color.

When using color theory to guide your decisions, think about the interactions that colors might have with your information. Slides have a design hierarchy, and color can complement or hinder this hierarchy. If you choose a dull or less visible color for the most important piece of information on the slide, you have made a mistake. Take a look at each slide and consider what captures your eye first. If the most important piece of information captures your eye, then you

have succeeded. There is no general rule for what colors are most memorable. You just need to consider that certain colors stand out against certain backgrounds and evoke different types of emotions. For example, a large bright-red block of text against a black background stands out more than does a light-yellow block of text against a white background.

Kenny's Tip

Sometimes lighting can completely change the colors on a slide. It's important to do a test to see how the colors appear in the actual venue. The audience may not see a bright blue, or a dark red might look black.

Color and Your Brand

When presenting on behalf of your company, you may have specific guidelines that determine how you use color in your presentation. You are an extension of your brand. Most companies put a lot of effort into making sure their print, digital, broadcast, and outdoor advertising are all brand cohesive, but many forget presentations. So keep in mind that you want to deliver a consistent experience, and one of the best times to do this is during a pitch.

At Big Fish Presentations, we work with many companies that adhere to brand guidelines, and we make sure that we represent their brands correctly. Delivering a consistent experience with your marketing materials, including presentations, helps your audience remember you and what your brand stands for.

It is also important to consider what you are speaking about. Microsoft and Apple product presentations have always been noted for their impact, maintaining consistent branding that matches the company's style. But Unilever COO Harish Manwani designed his presentation by focusing on the concept of social good rather than on Unilever. He used yellow as his focal color and not the company color, blue; this was perfect for his message. Think about the context of your presentation and whether it is appropriate to veer off and create a color scheme that is more reflective of your story than of your company.

Some of the best presentations ever delivered did not have a "cohesive brand experience." Use your best judgment.

VISUAL HIERARCHY

When most of us think of hierarchy, we associate the concept with a way of organizing people, placing them in a certain order according to their status or importance. In design, a hierarchy is defined as a "specific order of objects that are in a graded ranking, in which some objects are placed above others."[20] These hierarchies point to different relationships between objects and their levels of relative importance. Most organized presentations have a hierarchy of information: main points, subpoints, and supporting information. For our purposes, the function of hierarchy is to create visual order.

When making a slide, people tend to forget that the information they are displaying has a hierarchy. We take it for granted when our presentation templates have space for a title and supporting text. When we are faced with the task of organizing our slide in a meaningful way, we don't really consider all the factors that affect the hierarchy of our information. Graphic designers are taught to be mindful of this. We may not all be designers, but we can certainly employ some of their methods.

The hierarchy of text takes into account color, alignment, scale, weight, and spatial intervals.[21] Distinguishing colors can be used to place a level of importance on text or graphics. We talked about color in the last section and explored how a specific color chosen for an object or graphic can have psychological implications. Well, the relation of this color to other colors on the slide can also play an important role in the hierarchy. For example, let's say you are using dark-red text for all your main points. The red acts as a visual cue, letting the audience know when you are moving to your next point and what level of information you are discussing. Color can also distinguish less important information on a slide from more important information. Using a bright color for the most important word in a sentence will make it stand out from the rest of the sentence. The audience knows to accord a certain importance to that word.

Alignment, in the case of presentations, is often associated with the dreaded bullet point. A title is usually justified to the left of the other bullet points. This gives the audience a sense for what information is of the highest importance. While many hate bullet points, the concept of alignment differentiation among text or objects can be an important asset when designing a slide, especially when you want to distinguish sub-points from main points. Use bullet points wisely. A slide with 10 bullet points is much harder to grasp than a slide with one idea.

Scale and weight are two sides of the same coin. Scale involves the different levels of size between objects or text. Weight is usually associated with the boldness of text. This can mean using either two versions of one font or two different fonts to draw a distinction between pieces of text. There is a pretty simple equation that everyone understands: BIG = important; small = not as important. The bigger the text or object on the slide, the more visual importance it carries. The audience's eyes will be drawn to it first. Simple, right? You can use different sizes and weights to visually distinguish what the most and least important pieces of information are on a slide.

Finally, the spatial separation between objects or text can be a way to structure a hierarchy. Objects that are clustered together in groups will be associated with one another.

In our experience, hierarchy is one of the most overlooked concepts in presentation design. Many know how to use pictures, graphics, color schemes, and text in a presentation, but most do not know how to organize it all. In many of the worst presentations we have seen, most of the issues centered on either an overload of information or an inability to distinguish which information is important. As a presenter, you always want to make it easy for your audience. The less work your listeners have to do to understand your presentation, the more they are able to retain. Not that you don't want to make them think; you just don't want them sorting through your disorganized presentation to get to the heart of your message. A hierarchy can organize your information for your own benefit, but more important, it organizes your information for your audience's benefit.

The first tip for establishing hierarchy is simple: have one. The second is to execute it well. Without the presenter to give the information a frame of reference, different visual hierarchies can completely change what you are trying to say. Let's look at some of the ways you can develop a hierarchy. We discussed all the factors separately, but we really need to look at all of them together. Here are a few slides that display the same information in completely different ways:

What We Do
Storytelling
Design
Training
Video

EXAMPLE 1

All the text is the same size and weight and is aligned to the left.

WHAT WE DO
Storytelling
Design
Training
Video

EXAMPLE 2

Color, weight, and scale are used to draw a more distinct contrast between the title and the subpoints.

WHAT WE DO

Storytelling

Design

Training

Video

EXAMPLE 3

Here we utilize spatial separation between the title and the list to draw attention to the title first. The secondary-level information is indented, further differentiating it from the title.

What We do

STORYTELLING
DESIGN
TRAINING
VIDEO

EXAMPLE 4

Size, weight, and color are used to draw the viewer's eye to the list below the title. Everything is centered. The title captures your attention last.

WHAT WE DO

Storytelling

DESIGN

Training

Video

EXAMPLE 5

This slide uses color and scale to draw attention to one of the items in the list. It's a simple way to show the audience where you are in the presentation.

WHAT WE DO

Storytelling
Training

Design
Video

EXAMPLE 6

This slide utilizes spatial separation. Two items of the list are placed on one side of a vertical line, and the other two are on the other side. This arrangement makes the audience separate these into two groups, whether intentionally or unintentionally.

As you consider ways to differentiate between objects in your hierarchy, keep in mind that you don't need to use all the methods that we've illustrated. "To create an elegant economy of signals, try using no more than three cues for each level or break in a document."[22] Choose the techniques you will use throughout your presentation and stick to them so that your audience understands the hierarchy after the first few slides.

When you are making a slide, you have some influence over the order in which people read your text and the likelihood of retention. In the previous examples, the different hierarchies gave the information varying meanings, bestowed different levels of importance, or separated the information into distinct groups. Using some of these techniques to organize your information will strengthen your presentation. Plan what you want people to notice first and what you want them to remember the most. Visual hierarchy is just another way to manage the relationship that your design has with your audience, or your presentation aesthetic. Organize your information around this principle, and you will be one step ahead of many presenters.

TYPOGRAPHY

Your use of text and typography is more than just a decision about what looks good or not. These decisions can affect the ability of your audience to read a slide efficiently and grasp the information displayed. Here are a few suggestions to consider when making decisions about your typography.

Font

When you open up your presentation program, you choose either to use one of the preloaded themes with fonts or to specify the fonts you prefer. Fonts are a graphical means to stand out from the millions of presentations given every day. And we mean stand out in a good way.

On July 4, 2012, two topics were trending on the web, Higgs boson and Comic Sans. That day was an amazing one for physicists and a bad one for typography lovers. The scientists at CERN, the European Organization for Nuclear Research, had announced the discovery of the Higgs boson, or "God particle," a major discovery that would "open the door to an entirely new realm of physics."[23] The talk of the day for typography lovers was that the loathed font, Comic Sans, was used in the presentation that announced the discovery. The days that followed were filled with funny tweets and posts as screenshots of the presentation went viral. When people say that font choice doesn't really matter, tell them this story. While this brought news of the discovery to the attention of more people, it was all because of a bad font choice. Do yourself a favor. Don't be the butt of jokes; find a good font.

Fonts can also help you reinforce the theme or feel of the story you are telling. There are many different fonts, but let's focus on the two major styles, serif and sans serif. A serif font can be recognized by the short lines that are located at the end of the strokes of each letter. A traditional serif font can be used to give a more conservative feel to your type. Sans serif fonts lack these short lines. Sans serifs lend type a modern feel. They are also used for emphasis due to their readability. These family groupings of serif and sans serif don't necessarily always adhere to these general characteristics. The wide variety of fonts available give you options that can work for your specific presentation.

Which fonts should you use then? The presentation platform that you will be working with provides some initial options. Microsoft PowerPoint offers font options that are traditionally used in the rest of Microsoft Office. Prezi is a cloud-based presentation tool that has a set of handpicked fonts. You can certainly go out of your way to find other fonts that you want to use. This may take a little more time and may cause some formatting issues, but stepping out of the norm may help you stand out.

There are web resources that allow you to download custom fonts, such as UrbanFont, Lost Type, or FontSquirrel. However, custom fonts don't work on all presentation platforms, and the font must be downloaded on the computer you are using for the presentation. This simple oversight can cause slides to look slightly off because the font did not load properly. As long as you keep these issues in mind, a custom font can really help you stand out. Below is a list of some of Big Fish's favorite fonts, some paid for and some free:

——— PURCHASED ———

Futura

Gotham

Helvetica Neue

Avenir

Akzidenz-Grotesk Condensed

——— FREE ———

BEBAS NEUE

Roboto

Merriweather

FRANCHISE

Mission Gothic

There are thousands of fonts that you can choose from. If you are presenting on behalf of your company, choose the fonts that have been determined to represent your brand well. But if you have some creative freedom, be sure to use no more than three fonts in your entire presentation. Different font styles can help develop a hierarchy, but too many will confuse an audience. Simplicity is best.

Finally, bear in mind that a font plays a very important functional role. Its legibility is paramount. Choosing a legible font is a service to your audience. The point of the slide is to act as a reference for your presentation, or in other cases as the readers' primary guide through the information.

Text Size

Remember the terrible presentation that was the catalyst for Big Fish? Each slide had 20 bullets, was set in 8-point font, and contained a few hundred words. Never do this to your audience.

Many speakers rely on their slides as a crutch to make up for their lack of preparation. They will fill each slide with information so they can just read off it. When you stop using your slides as a crutch and think about the impact that your visuals can have on your audience,

you will realize that simplicity is always best. We'll show you what we mean with this example.

Solutions 1 and 2 are both valuable ways to break down your information into digestible pieces. But keep in mind that if you opt for solution 2, breaking up your slides will ultimately lead to a much larger presentation. This may be more difficult to pull off, but it will save the audience from information overload. Keep your slides to under 20 words. By limiting yourself to a word count, you make your message more impactful. Simplifying a complex idea to a small, easy-to-digest piece of information is one of the most valuable skills that a communicator can learn.

Another thing to note about the sample slides is the change in font size. The first slide has the smallest font size, while all the other slides employ a larger font size, about 30 points or greater, which makes it easier for your audience to read. As in font choice, legibility is paramount when determining font size.

There are situations where you may want to put a little more information on your slides, and that's OK. When a presentation is used as an informational document that will be sent to a group of people, the slides will not result in information overload if the audience has the time to sit and read through the deck. As well, more

Building Recognition

- The fonts that you have in your presentation can be the visuals that your audience remembers most.
- You want your audience to remember your company's brand.
- Good typography sets the tone for the entire presentation.
- Typography can be a memorable mark of your company.
- It can be the one thing the viewer identifies with time and time again.

EXAMPLE

This slide has 60 words in a small font. If you were sitting at a conference, would you spend the time to read any of this? No, and neither would anyone else. You want to pay attention to the speaker.

Building Recognition

(1) Fonts are memorable and can represent your brand. Let typography set the tone.

SOLUTION 1

Make a simple statement. Do the explaining rather than letting your slides do it for you.

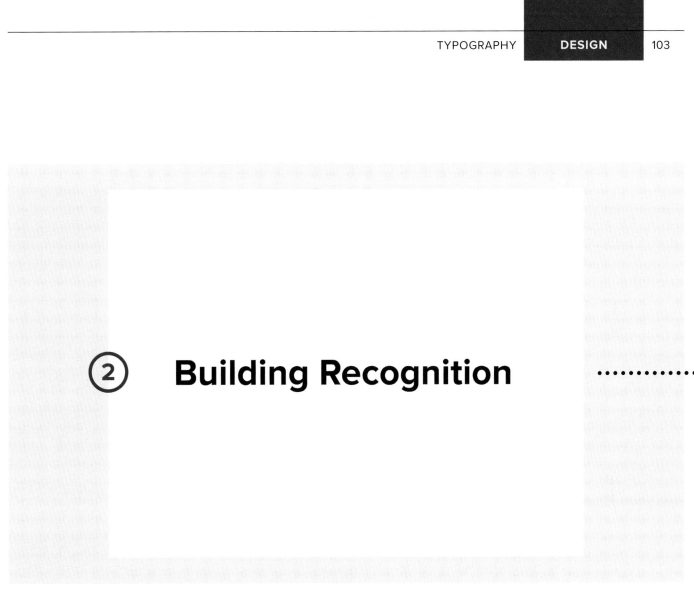

(②) **Building Recognition**

SOLUTION 2

Another technique is to break information down into smaller digestible bits.
Take a look at the next three slides.

(continues)

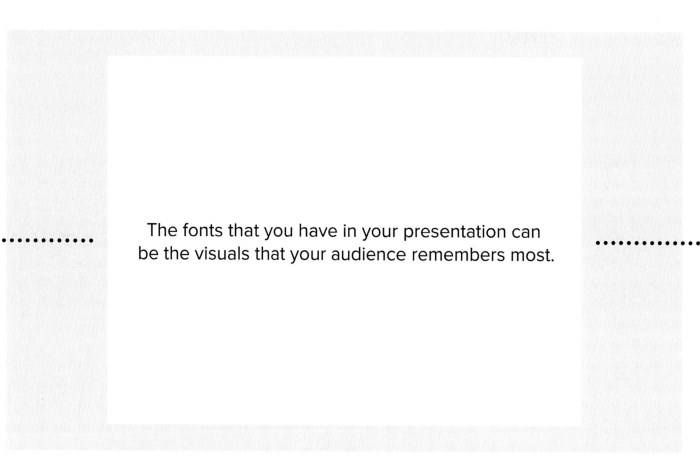

The fonts that you have in your presentation can be the visuals that your audience remembers most.

SOLUTION 2 *(continues)*

Each of the three main points is on its own slide. The speaker is able to explain each point in adequate time, while the audience focuses only on that point.

You want your audience to remember
your company's brand.

This may not always be easy for the speaker, but it's the easiest way for the audience to digest the information.

(continues)

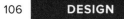

Good typography sets the tone
for the entire presentation.

SOLUTION 2 *(continues)*

It also decreases clutter and leaves room for memorable graphics or photos.

information on the slide may be beneficial when presentations will be viewed through a website such as SlideShare.[24] SlideShare is a site where people from all over the world can upload their presentations. It's the YouTube for presentations. When users browse through websites like these, readers have time to digest the information at their own pace. In both these cases, the slide deck is the focal point of information delivery. This is very different from an actual talk, where the speaker is the focal point.

Layout

In designing the layout of the text, consider the use of *white space* and the effect that *monotony* may have on your slides.

White space is the portion of your slide that isn't occupied by text, graphics, or photos. Use white space to keep your slides from feeling busy or cluttered. Utilizing empty or negative space, other terms for white space, on a slide also keeps you from making your text too large. Text that is too large can seem clunky and distracting to the viewer during a presentation. Empty space also gives your design a visual frame. Many use premade templates that have graphic elements that frame all the information on the slide. White space can be a very effective, simple, and clean way to achieve the same result.

Whereas white space can help the audience focus on important points, monotony—our second layout concern—is an attention killer.

Without poets, without artists, men would soon weary of nature's monotony.

—Guillaume Apollinaire

You can avoid monotony by not having the same predictable layout for all your slides. Be creative. Use a textual hierarchy to differentiate what you feel are the most important or impactful slides.

Switching it up will keep the audience engaged. Aim to make your audience wonder what the next slide might reveal.

———

By using white space judiciously and employing techniques to avoid monotony, you will create slides that are not only readable but also memorable.

ARTWORK

*Photography is the only language that can
be understood anywhere in the world.*

—BRUNO BARBEY

Photography

Photography is a transcendent way to tell amazing stories. And a single photograph has the potential to capture an entire story.

In 2011, the world was experiencing the Arab Spring. Revolutions across multiple countries occurred as citizens fought for freedom from despotism and tyranny. The photo on this spread was taken in the midst of the revolution in Cairo, Egypt, where Christians were protecting Muslims as they prayed. The photo illustrates solidarity between people of different faiths. It was used in reports across many news outlets throughout the West. This one photo symbolized an entire Egyptian revolution.

Powerful photos like this leave the audience with much more than just a feeling, but with an entire idea of a story and an experience. While not every photo in a presentation can be this impactful, this is a good example of how photography can help the presenter tell a story in a meaningful and memorable way.

Finding Photos

Good photos are hard to find. There are two ways to do it. The first is to go out and take them.

We aren't suggesting you become a professional photographer, but we love photos that are representative of your story and experiences. We feel that this can be a great addition to a presentation, because it can be a more immersive way to get your audience involved. This is not applicable to every type of presentation,

EGYPTIAN REVOLUTION

Tahrir Square, 2011
Nevine Zaki

but if you think creatively, you may be able to find scenarios that would be great to document as part of a presentation.

Scott Harrison, founder of Charity: Water, gives a presentation that is a terrific example of how photographs work to illustrate your story.[25] In his talk to LeWeb Paris in 2012, he tells the story of his major life change and the creation of Charity: Water. He talks about his past as a club promoter and illustrates this with photos

of himself during this time in his life. Then he describes an experience that changed his life. He had volunteered as a photographer in Africa and documented the deformities of those who were affected by tainted water. After seeing these horrific effects, he started Charity: Water. He documented, through photography, his experiences during this life transformation and the amazing work that his charity is doing to change the world. Although Scott is an amazing presenter and storyteller, it is his photographs that immersed his

Kenny's Tip

For corporate, sales, and investment presentations, I recommend using authentic photos taken by you or your brand instead of stock image photos. People buy from people. It's easier for the audience to relate to real people rather than random models in a staged shoot. Don't be afraid to show who you are.

audience in his story. We may not all be professional photographers, but we have the opportunity to document important experiences in our lives.

The other way to do it is to use another photographer's work, whether by asking a photographer directly or through outlets that sell stock photography. Searching the collections of stock photo houses can be a very time efficient and easy way to find good photos to use in a presentation. When you are preparing a talk and you have a million things on your mind, time is of the essence. However, there are a slew of issues that arise when stock photos are used incorrectly. Let's talk through some of the biggest mistakes and how you can remedy them.

Photo quality is something that many amateur presenters disregard when using photos. Many will find a photo through a search engine and then copy and paste it directly into their presentations. Not only is this an easy way to get in trouble for using someone else's photography without permission, but the resulting file can be low resolution and pixelated. The message is lost when people aren't able to see what the photo is trying to illustrate. The picture becomes a distraction when your audience members are struggling to figure out what you're showing them.

These two slides illustrate the difference that pixilation and low-quality photography can have on a presentation. Example 1 can be read easily, and the photo shows a beautiful landscape in Africa. Example 2 is so pixelated that it distorts the details of the picture. Low-quality photography can also undermine your credibility. It can imply that you didn't spend enough time finding adequate visuals or aren't meticulous in your work.

There are a few situations where pixelated or low-quality photos can be used and still be memorable. When you are using old photos to tell a story about your own experiences or touch on a historical moment, you don't need to dress up the images; the audience will understand why the pictures aren't of the best quality.

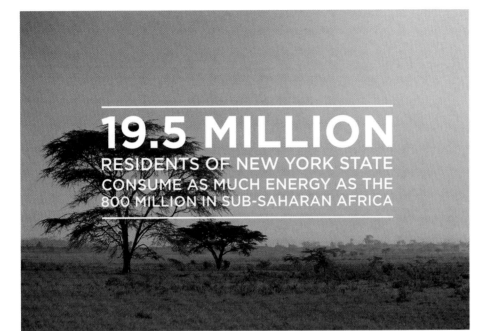

EXAMPLE 1

This slide uses a high-quality photograph.

EXAMPLE 2

The low-quality photograph distracts from the message.

Think back to one of the boring presentations that you've sat through. Remember the slide with the businessman holding out his hand for a handshake? How about the typical slide with the big thumbs up? Well, we remember those, too, and we have seen those same clichéd photos hundreds of times. Clichéd photography is rampant in marketing today. These are the same photos that you see on millions of small business websites and in amateur presentations. When finding your photos for a presentation, don't stick to what is expected. If you use the same photo that an audience has seen 100 times before, it is worse than using no photo at all. If you want to use a photograph, try not to represent the concept in a superficial way. Identify the core of what you want to say and don't use typical buzzwords.

Take a look at these two slides. Example 1 uses a stock photo that we have seen a million times. Do a quick search for the term "business growth," and it is one of the first photos that pop up. A finger rises above a typical business graph illustrating growth, with a map of the continents symbolizing new markets in the background. It is easily understood and is relevant, which is good. But it is tired.

But if Austin, Texas, represents the market in which you experienced the largest growth, then highlight it by using a photo of the city skyline, as in Example 2. It is simple and relevant but also specific to your presentation.

EXAMPLE 1

This is the epitome of clichéd photography.

EXAMPLE 2

This photo is more evocative.

When finding a photo, be wary of those that look too staged. We've all seen those images with a person or object against a white background. Staged photos can come across as inauthentic. At Big Fish, we love using photos of real experiences and real people who are part of the story, but these aren't always available. You can remedy this by using photography that seems more natural and easier for an audience to connect with.

With all these rules in mind, where do you find high-quality pictures? Big Fish uses stock photo websites such as iStock and Shutterstock (you will find more photo resources at the end of the book). They have thousands of original photos that can be used to stand out from the crowd.

Another relatively new asset that can help presenters find unique photos is Offset.[26] A subsidiary of Shutterstock, Offset is a new take on stock photos that includes a large collection that is curated by award-winning artists from all over the world. Although pricier than some other options, the website includes a database of beautiful photographs that can help presenters tell their stories through photography.

Two tools that are great for those in the software or social media industry are uiFaces and Placeit. UiFaces is a website that provides avatar photos for user interface mockups as well as live websites (commercial use only available from their authorized section).[27] This is a way to get "real" people rather than the typical stock photo style for your presentations. You may use these avatar photos for product demo presentations or social networking presentations. Placeit is great for app developers who need to place screenshots of applications or websites in photos of frames, tablets, or computers.[28] This is a quick and beautiful way to do it without having to use difficult design programs.

EXAMPLE 1

This photo is obviously staged.

EXAMPLE 2

This photo conveys a more realistic and natural tone.

Using Photos

You decided to replace your clichéd clip art with an awesome picture. Or you had a large amount of information but instead chose a photo to convey the same concept. These are good first steps. A presenter can find an engaging photo for a slide, but he or she can also undermine the impact of the photo by using it incorrectly. When featuring photography in a presentation, we like to keep a few important factors in mind.

PLACEMENT AND FRAMES

Many presenters just drop the photo on the slide without any thought. It's just there. We like to give it some purpose. One way to do this is by simply adding a frame around it. A frame visually retains the photo and makes it easier on the eyes. Take a look at the first two examples. Both have the same great photo, but the slide with the framed photo appears more intentional. Many of the well-known presentation platforms have frame options that allow you to do this. We like to say that it gives the photo a sense of purpose, that you meant for it to be there.

Another way to place a photo on a slide is by using a full bleed. "Full bleed" is a design term that means placing the image so it fills the entire space right up to the edges. This enables the audience to see the details of the photo. You should do this if seeing the details will enhance understanding and if the photo is an important talking point during the presentation.

EXAMPLE 1

Photo without a frame

EXAMPLE 2

Photo with a frame

EXAMPLE 3

Slide with a full-bleed photograph

INTERACTION WITH OTHER PHOTOS OR TEXT

One of our biggest design pet peeves is slide clutter. "We have 20 great pictures from this event for the presentation. Let's put them all on one slide." Just like information overload, presenters can create a slide that has image overload. Time and time again we run into people who love their pictures and would rather put 10 decent photos on a slide instead of just one great photo. No one can see all the photos adequately, which takes the beauty and impact away from each individual picture. If all the photos are incredibly important, spread them over multiple slides. If the pictures are not completely necessary, choose the best one that reflects what you are trying to get across. The audience will be able to see all of what is in the photo and appreciate how you are using it to tell your story.

EXAMPLE 1

This slide has too many photos.

Combining text with photography is another tricky area. In this case, you need to watch out not for image overload, but for information overload. Be careful that your slide design doesn't undermine the audience's ability to understand the slide, decreasing its impact and creating distraction.

When using text on a slide, with or without a photo, keep the information to a minimum. This is especially important when placing large amounts of text over a photo. The text isn't just creating information overload; it's becoming a visual distraction that is difficult to read.

EXAMPLE 2

Use just one photo to convey your message.

THE RULE OF THIRDS

One of the most important principles is the rule of thirds.[29] This consists of dividing the photo into a grid of nine sections, split by three horizontal lines and three vertical lines. When you split the photo or slide into sections, there are points on the slide that tend to pull visual focus. Use these points as a guide to place text on your slide, knowing that the audience's eyes will be drawn to that area of the slide. Take a look at the two examples and how they use the rule of thirds.

EXAMPLES

Two good examples of how photographers draw the eye using the rule of thirds.

EXAMPLE 1

This slide uses an icon that is too complicated.

EXAMPLE 2

Using simple icons enhances comprehension.

Icons

Another great tool to convey an idea with artwork is an icon or a graphic. Like photography, icons can replace cheesy clip art or large amounts of text. An icon is a graphic way to represent a concept or idea.

Most of our suggestions about photography also relate to icons: they should be high quality, authentic, relevant. But we have one more: keep it simple. Many make the mistake of using an icon that is too complicated, which dilutes the power of their message.

You may find icons and graphics on all the major stock photography websites that we have mentioned. But some are in vector format for designers. And if you aren't a designer, it is difficult to get a good-quality icon using these file types. A free tool for nondesigners and designers alike is Captain Icon,[30] which gives the user free access to 350 icons that can be downloaded in png and vector formats. Another is Iconion.[31] This nifty tool allows nondesigners to create different types of icons using specific design styles for their presentations. Prezi also has a great library of simple icons that can be used within the program. Remember to consider functionality and simplicity, and make sure what you choose will work with the program you are using.

MOTION

Animation

Wouldn't it be awesome if everyone were as talented as a Pixar animator? Imagine your presentation being as captivating as *Toy Story* or *Finding Nemo*. But the truth is we aren't, and neither are you (well, unless you are actually an animator at Pixar). Animating parts of your presentation can make it more engaging, which will make you stand out. Animation can improve your presentation aesthetic, which helps your audience comprehend what you are trying to say. There are hundreds of different animation combinations that you can use in presentation platforms such as Keynote and Power-Point, and some, like Prezi, utilize motion in a completely different way. We'll go over a few of our favorite animation examples as well as touch on some big no-nos.

PROCESS

We believe in taking something complicated and breaking it down to its simplest and most digestible form. When you're able to simplify and use animation to help illustrate each step of a process, you will make it easier to comprehend.

Let's say you have a complicated process that you have simplified into a flowchart or process visual. One way to illustrate this is to animate each piece of your process individually as you're talking about each step. Once you're done, the audience can see the steps that you took and the final outcome all in one flow.

Using animation to illustrate a process or timeline makes a slide more impactful.

PROCESS 1

This animation shows how the presence of one store . . .

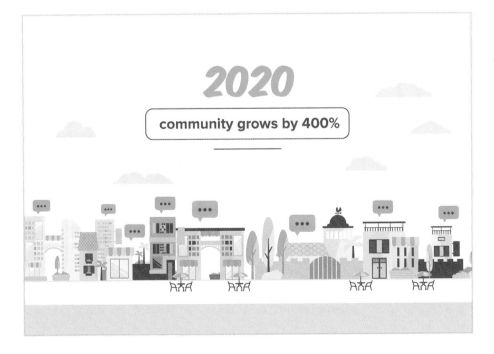

PROCESS 2

. . . stimulates the growth of a community.

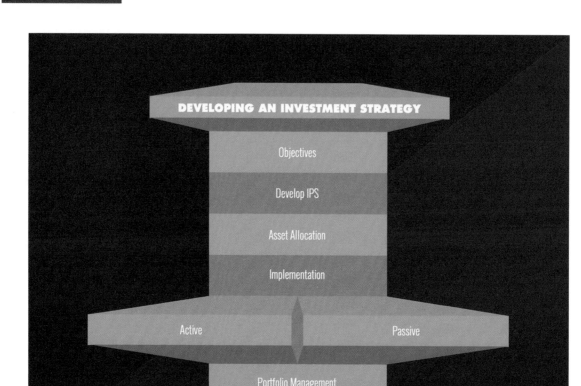

CONTRAST 1

If you have a list or a group of objects, using animation to show contrast draws focus to a specific point.

CONTRAST

Use animation to show important contrasts in your information. For example, let's say you have a list of the most important goals of an initiative. Use animation and the tools that you learned in the hierarchy section to highlight each point as you discuss it. Change the color, size, and spacing to make the information stand out.

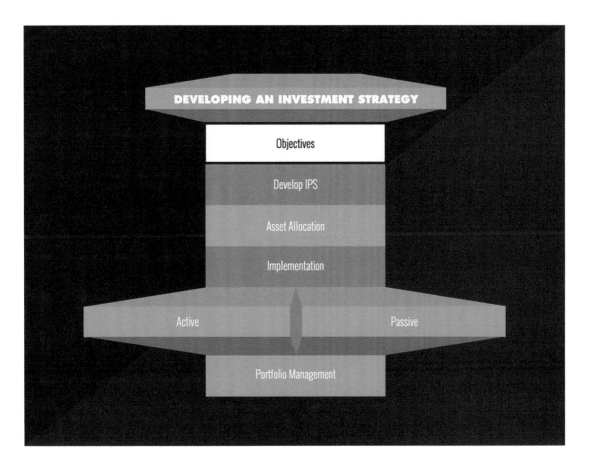

CONTRAST 2

This slide highlights the talking point in a different color. This lets the audience know where to focus.

REVEAL 1

This is a screenshot of the Prezi we created for Big Fish. The fish represent ideas.
The net is a metaphor for how Big Fish combines and refines these ideas.

REVEAL

The big reveal. This is something that we love to do using the presentation platform Prezi. It's a graphic way to walk your audience through some slides and then zoom out to show them the "big picture." Other

presentation platforms can illustrate reveals, but the canvas style of Prezi really allows you to do this in an engaging way. In a Prezi we created for ourselves, we used fish as a metaphor for ideas. We showed a few fish

REVEAL 2

We zoom out and up to reveal that Big Fish is working to catch all these great ideas.
The Prezi platform is ideal for the big reveal.

caught in a net. Then we zoomed out to reveal that the net is being drawn by a ship that represents Big Fish. We started with a specific element and zoomed out to show the whole picture.

Keep it simple and be intentional. Enhance your story. While we remember the amazing animation that Pixar produces, we remember their beautiful stories even more. Animation is just a way to tell stories.

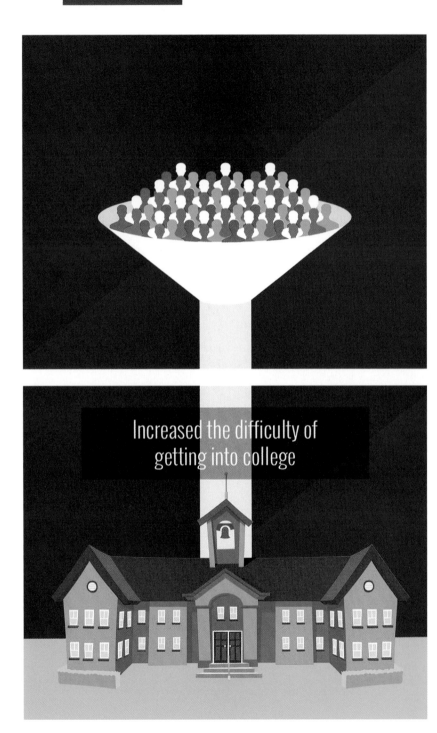

Increased the difficulty of getting into college

Transitions

Swoosh—explosion—blam: now read this chart. Have you seen a version of these transitions in a presentation? Bad slide transitions have been annoying audiences since the 2000s.

We are partial to *fade* and *push* transitions when using platforms such as PowerPoint and Keynote. Fades are a simple, yet elegant, way to transition from one slide to the next. Sometimes in film, a director chooses a fade over a hard cut to create a smooth transition to the next scene. It's the same basic principle. The push transition treats the next slide as a continuation of the previous slide.

TRANSITIONS

The first slide sets up the concept and uses a push-down transition to give the illusion that the slides are one continuous piece of art.

Distractions

We have seen hundreds of presenters who use transitions and animation that eventually work against them by becoming distractions from the message. To prevent this, ask yourself two questions.

IS THIS TOO MUCH?

Let's say you have five design elements on a slide: a title and two pieces of text each surrounded by a box. You want to animate each element, one after the other. This doesn't sound too bad, but let's say you do this for 20 slides. So five animated elements multiplied by 20 slides equals 100 animated pieces in your presentation. That's too much. If you want people to pay attention to your talk but you have 100 animated elements behind you, realize that their attention will be drawn from what you are saying to the distractions behind you. Use animation sparingly and carefully. It is very easy to visually overload the audience.

The same goes for transitions. Do not use a transition for every slide. Review your presentation and make sure that the focus is on what you are trying to communicate and not on how your slides swoosh from one to the next.

IS THIS OVER THE TOP?

If you have never asked yourself this question, the answer is probably yes. Presentation platforms offer many options for simple and visually pleasing transitions and animation, but they also have a lot of bad ones. Stay away from over-the-top 3D animation transitions and animation that is too complex.

Kenny's Tip

If you can't decide on the right blend of transitions, do away with them entirely. You lower the risk of complicating your slide deck and detracting from its intended purpose. If your presentation is already well designed, people won't miss the transitions.

Video

People love videos. As presenters find ways to continuously engage their audiences, we have witnessed a sharp increase in the use of videos in presentations. We see them in global product launches, small sales presentations, inspirational speeches—you name it. When you see Apple open with a beautiful brand video about the new iPhone before the presenter comes on-stage, you wonder how you can use video to captivate your audience.

Like photos, there are really only two ways to get videos for your presentation: create one or use someone else's. Either way, there are a few things to keep in mind when using a video in your talk.

YOU ARE TAKING THE FOCUS AWAY FROM YOURSELF

This can be OK if it helps make your point and if you feel comfortable breaking your flow. Make sure to keep your videos very brief, and check to see that your audience is still engaged. It's not impossible to make an amazing presentation while using a 10-minute video, but we wouldn't advise it.

TIMING IS EVERYTHING

The best use of videos has been as a powerful opener or as a strong closer. A powerful opener can set the tone for the rest of your presentation and can help your audience stay engaged. When you close with a video, remember that it is the last thing you are leaving with your audience. Make sure it counts.

It's true that great presenters don't have to limit their use of video to the beginning or end, but be very cautious when using video in the middle. It may break your momentum and make it difficult to jump back into the talk. Decide what works best with your flow.

MAKE SURE IT'S RELEVANT

If you are having a video made specifically for the presentation, you may not need to worry about this. But if you are using someone else's content, there is a greater chance the video may be slightly off-topic. Make sure that whatever videos you choose are relevant to your subject and enhance what you are saying.

APPEAL TO THE EMOTIONS AND CONSIDER BEAUTY

Curate your videos carefully. Like photos, videos can pack a powerful punch while delivering important information.

Beauty is not just about the quality of the footage or the crispness of the graphics. Be creative. During the 2012 Google I/O conference, instead of showing a branded video to showcase Google Glass, the company videoconferenced with a group of skydivers who were wearing Google Glass as they were diving directly into the venue. When you think outside the box, you can use video in a way that creates a memorable experience for your audience.

Videos and Delivery

Kenny learned firsthand how important it is to prepare when using video in your delivery. He had made the decision to use a prerecorded video that he would interact with as he was being introduced on stage. It would seem like he was video-chatting with the person who was introducing him. It was a pretty cool idea—in theory. He learned two important lessons:

- *Rehearse.* When you use video, make sure to practice how to transition between the video and your talk.

- *Consider the venue.* This is a biggie. You may not always be able to see where you are presenting beforehand, but you really need to try to. If Kenny had seen the venue before his talk, he would have known that he would be walking into the room at an awkward angle from the video and that the screen was a little too small for the entire audience to see. When these mishaps occur, the awesome video you planned on showing ends up being a momentum killer, leaving the audience uncomfortable.

In the event of a mishap, adapt. Kenny took it in stride and charged ahead with his presentation. Great presenters learn to adapt their material (content, design, delivery) to any situation, putting ego aside to make the necessary changes for maximum impact.

Kenny's Tip

When using video in your presentation, think beyond PowerPoint and Keynote. I use a video file of a fully animated Big Fish logo on my opening slide (when you own a presentation company, people expect to be wowed). By adding small video elements, you can create a presentation that seems to have pieces of animation that would be impossible in a typical PowerPoint. Not a motion artist or videographer? No problem! Websites such as Animoto (easy) and Animatron (more difficult but allows for greater customization) are great tools that will help you create animated video clips.

DATA

Data Is Everywhere

We talked about data earlier when we discussed crafting your content. We touched on how to transform your data from mere statistics to something relevant, something that can evoke emotion. In this section, we're going to show you how to turn your raw data into an impactful image. We're going to talk about making data mean something.

Data is everywhere. We consume data all the time and in many forms. Every retweet, "like," status update, and shared news article is a piece of data. For those who try to use data to make a difference, it has become increasingly important to visualize it.

Many of the presentations that are delivered today are based on or involve data. A CEO presenting first-quarter results, a young entrepreneur pitching his next big idea to a venture capitalist, an ad agency talking about audience reception of its client's new commercial—all are appealing to people's *logos*, or reason. Each presenter wants to show the audience the facts and persuade them through logic. Using statistics is an effective way to do this, but it's not the only way to persuade. People need to be able to show this information in a visual way. We don't want our audience simply to understand the data. We want them to understand the story behind the data. This is where data visualization comes in.

Visualizing Your Data

How would you take a collection of recent tweets and turn them into a compelling graphic that shows the most talked-about news in 2014? Well, you can make a chart, graph, tree map, or some other visual representation that can turn that data into something easily digestible for the audience.

In his 2010 TED talk about data visualization, David McCandless talks about making your information mean something.[32] He opens the talk with the idea that billions of dollars are being spent all across the world, and no one seems to know how to put numbers this large into something everyone can understand. He uses this beautiful tree map to show important statistics that aren't easily understood. The map shows

Billion-Dollar-O-Gram, graphic courtesy of Information Is Beautiful. Data visualization has been cropped: see full image at InformationIsBeautiful.net.

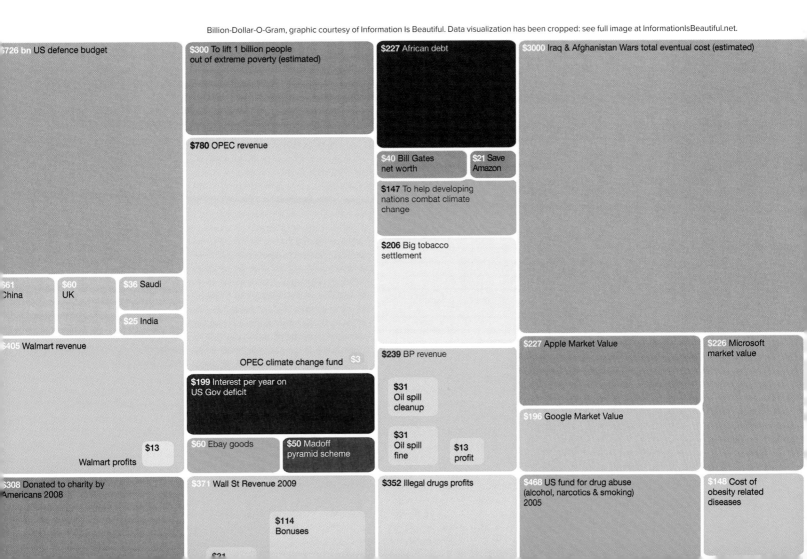

that the United States donates over $300 billion to foreign countries, which you can quickly compare with the $120 billion donated by the top 17 industrialized nations combined. The tree map includes other notable billions that have been discussed in the media, so you don't just see the numbers; you see how large they are in relation to each other.

"We need relative figures that are connected to other data so that we can see a fuller picture, and then that can lead to us changing our perspective," says David McCandless. This is what presenters try to do. We try to make a difference with our stories; we try to change an audience's perspective.

Charts, Graphs, and Other Things That Don't Sound Awesome

What are some of the ways we can turn our data into visuals that look awesome and mean something? As presenters, we have the typical tools to organize data: PowerPoint, Excel, Pages, and Numbers. We can choose the type of visualization we use: bar graphs, line graphs, pie charts, etc. We don't make our decisions based on what looks prettiest; we make our choices based on what presents our data best.

Here are some suggestions for using each major type.

BAR GRAPH

Bar graphs are great at showing proportions when comparing a few different data sets. Let's take a look at some data that plays a central role in our society today: funny animal videos.

This bar graph makes it very clear that cat videos are the most popular of the funny animal videos (but we already knew that). Bar graphs can also illustrate trends and the differences in these trends across time and other factors—but other graphs illustrate trends more clearly.

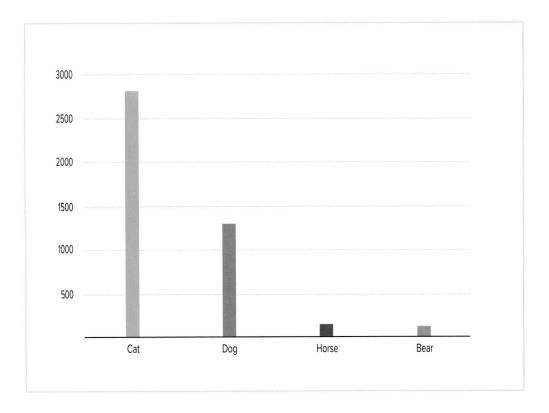

BAR GRAPH

The number of Google searches for cat, dog, horse, and bear videos in 2013.

LINE GRAPH

Line graphs are better at illustrating trends because they do not show you the individual points of data, in a way, perhaps, a bar graph would. Line graphs are meant to show you the relationships that all the points have with each other across a variable, such as time.

This chart looks at the same animal-video data as before, but it illustrates the trends over time. The previous bar graph depicted the number of searches among the various kinds of animal videos and showed that cat videos were most popular. The periods of time were not important. Here, it is the relationship between all these periods relative to each other. We see again that cats and dogs get a lot more love than animals that aren't typical pets. And for some reason, cats get even more popular during the holiday season (most likely because they are super cute in little holiday sweaters).

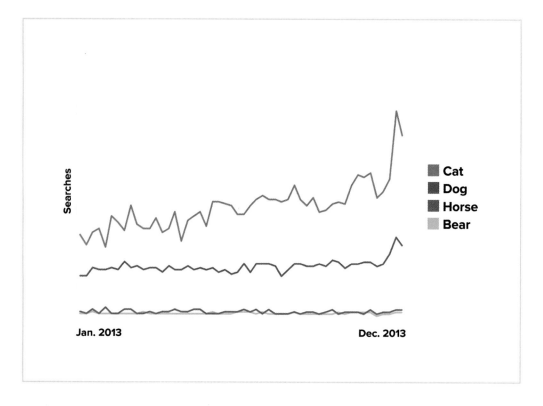

LINE GRAPH

This illustrates the data from January to December 2013.

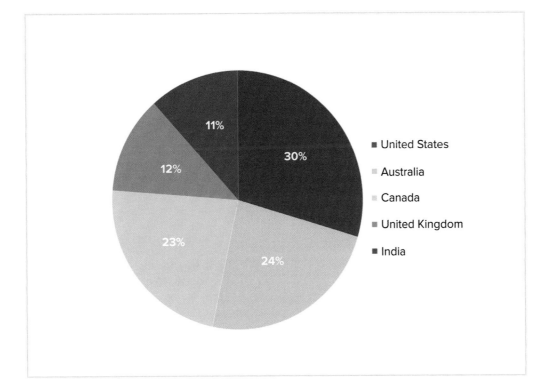

PIE CHART

The percentage of total searches by country.

PIE CHART

A pie chart is used when comparing proportions in a data set. You can take a complete sample of something and break it down into its constituent pieces.

Here, we break down the data into percentage of total searches by country. We can manipulate our data and present the information in many different ways.

OTHERS

Using a tree map is another great way to show proportions and put values into perspective. Tree maps aren't typically in presentation platforms, but there are add-ons to Microsoft Office and websites that help you make them. Another great way to view data is by using geographic visualizations. You can spread your data points across maps to show locations or proportions of data by location.

This visual shows you the Google search interest for funny cat videos by region, where the darker regions represent the greater number of searches.

Flowcharts are another way to illustrate a process. Just as a graph is meant to take large amounts of data and make the data digestible, a flowchart can be used to make complex processes more comprehensible.

Test your options to make sure that you are choosing the best way to visually represent your data. Ask yourself: "Does this chart represent what I am trying to say?"

GEOGRAPHIC VISUALIZATION

This shows the audience where the bulk of the cat-video searches were made.

The Age of Infographics

Turning data into beautiful visualizations that inspire and create change is more important than ever. We live in an age of accelerated media. It's not just about the quality of what you put out there; it's how quickly you are able to do so. This has contributed to the rise of infographics.

Visual.ly, a leading infographics blog, describes infographics as follows:[33]

- Visualizations that present complex information quickly and clearly

- Visualizations that integrate words and graphics to reveal information, patterns, or trends

- Visualizations that are easier to understand than words alone

- Visualizations that are beautiful and engaging

We like to point out an important word: "quickly." Infographics are ways to *quickly* describe patterns and trends seen in data. Presenting your information in this style is ideal. It enhances the audience's ability to remember the information.

ECONOMIC IMPACT
OF LOUISIANA BEER INDUSTRIES

DIRECT IMPACT	
(BREWING, DISTRIBUTING & RETAIL)	
JOBS	19,560
WAGES	$546,709,700
CONTRIBUTION	$1,223,176,400

$2,991,994,200
IN TOTAL ECONOMIC CONTRIBUTIONS

INDUSTRY-RELATED JOBS IN LOUISIANA (BY THOUSANDS)

AGRICULTURE	910
BUSINESS & PERSONAL SERVICES	4,380
CONSTRUCTION	200
FINANCE INSURANCE & REAL ESTATE	1,640
MANUFACTURING GENERAL	640
RETAIL	1,440
TRANSPORTATION & COMMUNICATION	1,010
TRAVEL & ENTERTAINMENT	1,440
WHOLESALE	440
OTHER	790

12,890
TOTAL INDUSTRY-RELATED JOBS IN LOUISIANA

TOP RATED BREWS

6.5%
ALCOHOL BY VOLUME

SERVE IN TULIP

NOLA HOPITOULAS IPA
INDIA PALE ALE (IPA)

This brew is the culmination of over 30 years of brewing by the Brewmaster, Peter 'Hopzilla' Caddoo. Created at the Tchoupitoulas Street brewery, this India Pale Ale was hand crafted with six malts and six hops. This big, beautiful beer is dry hopped with Amarillo and Simcoe hops to accentuate aromas of citrus and pine. Grab a Hopitoulas and taste the passion and dedication that has gone into this brew.

NOLA'S TOP 3	
HOPITOULAS IPA	3.51
IRISH CHANNEL STOUT	3.38
BROWN ALE	3.21
(RATED OUT 5 POSSIBLE POINTS)	

8%
ALCOHOL BY VOLUME

SERVE IN SNIFTER

ABITA SELECT IMPERIAL LOUISIANA OYSTER STOUT
IMPERIAL STOUT

This brew is made with pale, caramel, roasted and chocolate malts. Added oats give the beer a fuller and sweeter taste. The roasted malts give it dark color as well as its intense flavor and aroma. Flavors of toffee and chocolate are prevalent but not overpowering. Since the beer gets so much flavor from the malts there is not a lot of hop flavor. Freshly shucked Louisiana oysters are added to the boil, so the salt from the oysters gives the beer a great aroma and mouthfeel.

ABITA'S TOP 3	
SELECT IMPERIAL LA OYSTER STOUT	3.35
SPRING IPA	3.34
SAVE OUR SHORE (SOS)	3.31
(RATED OUT 5 POSSIBLE POINTS)	

Infographics are great, right? But they seem complicated and difficult to create for anyone who isn't a designer. There are many companies that produce infographics (*hint:* one of those companies wrote this book). But these businesses aren't really accessible to everyone, and an infographic takes time to create.

There are a few ways that anyone can integrate the principles of infographics into a data visualization.

CONSIDER SOMETHING OTHER THAN A GRAPH OR JUST WORDS

For example, you have data about your company's market share in the mobile phone industry. Let's say your company currently accounts for 60 percent of the market. Instead of creating the typical pie chart, maybe illustrate this in terms of phones. This is a simple way to cut out the usual, redundant line of text. You are able to present the statistic in terms of the actual object. By employing this technique, you can replace certain pieces of your presentation with infographics.

USE AN INFOGRAPHIC TO SHOW A PROCESS

Many use flowcharts that show relationships among groups and accomplish this beautifully. You can change things up by using real-world comparisons such as people or objects rather than the typical circles and rectangles.

CHOOSE ONE OF THE MANY ONLINE TOOLS THAT HELP NONDESIGNERS CREATE INFOGRAPHICS FROM THEIR DATA

Sites such as Piktochart, Plot.ly, and Infogr.am enable you to create beautiful infographics and include tools such as geographic visualizations, tree maps, and other useful charts and graphs.

USE OTHER DESIGNERS' INFOGRAPHICS THAT DEAL WITH YOUR TOPIC

There are many sites, such as visual.ly, that have amazing infographics you can use. If you are creating presentations within industries such as tech or healthcare, there are thousands of infographics online that highlight important statistics in these industries.

———

Infographics are a great tool. They turn your data into an engaging and memorable visual. They are a powerful way to use your presentation aesthetic to appeal to people's hearts and minds.

INFOGRAPHIC 1

A traditional way to illustrate a statistic. This style is simple and very easy for the audience to understand.

INFOGRAPHIC 2

Infographics like this can help put things into perspective for the audience. It can provide a frame of reference and a different way to look at the information.

HANDOUTS

Simple is always best when it comes to presentations. But we know that there are topics that require a heavy load of information. Cramming all of it on slides, even spread across many, is never the answer. If you need to cover a lot of information but don't want your slides to be unbearable, use handouts as a supplement.

Think of handouts as a separate element of your presentation, not a clone of it. This means that they shouldn't just be replicas of your slides. If the handouts and the presentation say the exact same thing, one of them is going to be forgotten. Instead, handouts should provide information that your audience didn't get in the presentation or that was too detailed for them to remember. Using handouts is a great way for you to cut down on the amount of clutter on your slides while still enabling the audience to see the information.

Handouts are also a good way to leave your audience with a tangible piece of your presentation. They're an extension of your message that stays with your audience long after the presentation.

We recommend passing out handouts after the presentation unless they are needed for an engaging activity or workshop. During the presentation, you want the attention to be on you, not on a piece of paper. If you split the attention between you and a handout, you run the risk of losing your audience's interest.

Having a handout doesn't mean you should go overboard. Include clean, readable copy, in-depth charts and graphs, price breakdowns, case studies, references, contact information, etc. The handout is your chance to elaborate in a way that you can't during your presentation, whether that is due to time constraints or just the sheer amount of information.

Here's an example of a situation where a handout could be used.
The first slide illustrates the clutter that most people include in their slides. After moving
the nitty-gritty details to a handout, we were able to make the slide a lot cleaner.

FIRST SLIDE

6 THINGS FROM OUR EXPERIENCE

Everything happens at 1000 mph! Our people were on the phone for 6-8 hours the first few days talking with FSIS, customers, the public. "It Takes a Village" & it is important to do no finger pointing. - SMA, Bobby Palesano, Dennis Johnson... OUR HEROES!!!

Set up a HOTLINE. Designate someone to handle all media calls and the hundreds of calls from the public! List that person's name and contact info in the FSIS Recall Notice. -Create a Recall Website... www.mandafinemeats.com (view our recall information). Post information and update continually for the benefit of the media and the public. Include a TIMELINE.

The unexpected... Having to "educate" our product liability insurance company's point person handling potential illness claims.

Public Relations Firm: You need to already know who will handle this. This firm, or person, should know your company well so that they can reflect your values when working your recall.

Routinely make sure that "ALL" customer contact info is UP-TO-DATE in your computer system. (Customer's name, Buyer/Contact name, address, phone number, e-mail address, and fax number).

Have a prioritized list of customers to be contacted, based on volume purchases from your company. Document when you notify customers. When fsis did their verifying, some customers said we never notified them, even when we had. We did have the proof.

HANDOUT

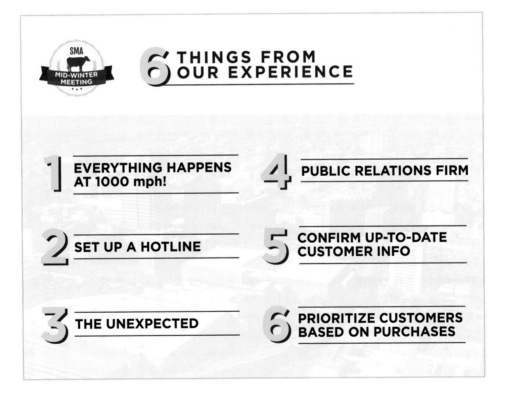

SECOND, MUCH CLEARER SLIDE

Avoid complex ideas that require extensive explanation and emotional stories that should be delivered in person. Don't expect the handout to do all the dirty work. This is especially true when it comes to communicating the main points of your presentation. Handouts are great tools to use in any presentation, but if you want something done right, you have to do it yourself.

Stylistically, handouts should match your presentation to provide a feeling of cohesiveness. If the whole point of providing a handout is to serve as an extension of your brand, then it should be designed in a similar fashion.

Although you may not be a master designer or even consider yourself artistically inclined, it is important that you design your handout to be easily readable and pleasing to the eye. If you don't feel confident about your own design skills, hire a firm or freelancer to create the design. It's worth the investment. In general, keeping it clean and simple will get you by, but being aesthetically interesting will take you above and beyond. Think about what you would personally like to see in a handout. You don't want to have an audience member share anything that you wouldn't want to read yourself.

Kenny's Tip

Great handouts are a part of the presentation experience. If you'd prefer to drive your audience to a digital version of your handout (to save time on printing and binding), you can give people a link to a PDF, a microsite, or push cards with the URL. One tool I recommend is Flowvella, which can create interactive PDFs in which you can embed videos and organize your content into sections.

TOOLS BEYOND POWERPOINT

Presentation ≠ PowerPoint

Ever since the first PowerPoint presentation was delivered in ancient Greece, PowerPoint has been the universal go-to application for presentations. OK, it wasn't in ancient Greece, but it sure feels like a while ago. PowerPoint has been so closely associated with presentations that many just assume that a presentation is a PowerPoint. This wouldn't be an issue if people throughout the world present well. But the truth is, they don't.

Because this world is plagued with bad presenters, and these offenders often use PowerPoint, it has gotten a bad rap. We've all heard of "death by PowerPoint."[34] Many think it's the program's fault. We don't think

that's the case. We love PowerPoint for a lot of reasons, and we want to dispel this unfair stigma. There are a lot of great presentation platforms out there, and bad presenters will continue to overload slides, present for too long, and ruin the experience for the audience. Don't blame an application for a person's mistake.

As more presentation platforms begin to emerge, we have more options, and presenters are able to choose what works best for them and for their audiences. Here are the most popular.

PowerPoint

Our favorite aspect of PowerPoint is intricacy. Power-Point has been a presentation platform for decades, and Microsoft has added incredible design tools that allow PowerPoint pros to really maximize what the program has to offer. For our purposes, the very detailed features of animation and design help us create presentations for clients that are very different from the everyday PowerPoint presentations that people usually see. That said, PowerPoint can be easy to overcomplicate with animation, transitions, and other features that may distract from your presentation.

Steve Jobs's Keynote

It might as well be called Steve Jobs's Keynote because it was originally built for just one user: Steve Jobs.[35] Jobs was well known for his very particular sense of design. His team at Apple created the program for him to use for his presentations at important conferences, and now anyone can use it, too.

WHAT WE LIKE

- *Design.* Keynote's interface is clean, and many of the stock options for graphics are minimalist. These existing graphics are great for amateur presenters who have no experience with more complicated design programs.

- *Not number one.* Because Keynote isn't the number one presentation platform, a lot of its features

haven't been overused. Keynote has a different set of fonts, textures, transitions, and animations, and these are in line with the simple, elegant Apple aesthetic.

- *Easy to learn.* If you are a presenter who has been using PowerPoint for years, using Keynote should be easy. The two platforms have major differences, but someone who understands the basics of PowerPoint should be able to understand the basics of Keynote.

THINGS TO KEEP IN MIND

Be sure to check for compatibility. PowerPoint has versions that work on Windows computers and Apple computers. Keynote is made only for Mac. We have had clients who created a presentation with animation and transitions in Keynote but then were unable to preserve full functionality when they had to convert the file to PowerPoint. We have also heard the horror story of the presenter who brought his Keynote on a USB, only to find out that the computer he was presenting on was a PC, not a Mac. He ended up having to present on the fly without his prepared deck. You can avoid this by bringing your own computer.

Prezi, the Zooming Presentation Tool

Big Fish has been using Prezi since 2010, just months after its release in 2009.

We have seen amazing growth in Prezi's customer base. There are now over "40 million people and 80% of Fortune 500 companies" using the product.[36] Being a Prezi Experts company, we'd love to help Prezi continue this growth throughout the world (see prezi.com/experts for more info). Prezi is a nonlinear platform that allows the presenter to build her entire presentation on one canvas and guide her audience through her talk by zooming through, in, and out of the information. Let's take a look at some of our favorite aspects of using Prezi.

Kenny's Tip

If you've never seen a Prezi, check out our very own Big Fish Prezi here: http://prezi.com/koevlyzxpqki/big-fish-prezi/.

PREZI ZOOM EXAMPLE

To keep the title screen simple and clean, we utilized the zooming ability of Prezi to cleverly hide all the slides within the symbol.

Think **EXAMPLE** *or* **PATTERN.**

WHAT WE LIKE

- *Create.* When you design a presentation in other applications, you look at each slide as an individual piece of information. When you work in Prezi, you are able to illustrate how pieces of information relate to each other. You may see connections that you might not have realized before. It's a digital mind map. We mentioned Prezi earlier as a good tool for storyboarding presentations. It enables you to focus on how everything flows together rather than on just each individual point.

- *Zoom.* The zooming aspect is what makes a Prezi a Prezi. The zoom is an engaging way to walk your audience through a story. It's a great way to navigate through information. Because Prezi is a digital mind map, it puts your audience a little inside your head and enables them to connect with your message. Although Prezi has been gaining in popularity, it is still not as ubiquitous as PowerPoint or Keynote. Using Prezi may help you stand out from the millions of PowerPoints or Keynotes that are delivered.

  We've talked about the big reveal, which is something we love at Big Fish. Prezi is a terrific way to showcase the big reveal. You take the audience through parts of the story and then reveal the big picture and what it all means. For example, let's say you have a new product with a dozen awesome features, but the real selling point is how all the features work together. You can walk the audience through each of the individual features and then zoom out to show how they are all connected. The big reveal is a fun technique to maintain suspense and keep your audience engaged.

- *Cloud.* Prezi is both a cloud-based and a desktop application. This means that you can create, save, and share your presentations on the go and on any computer. Modern-day presenters needn't worry about keeping a USB stick with them. With Prezi, they can make changes and present, using their iPad or any computer. Being on the cloud also allows for Prezi to function as a great collaboration tool. If you are working on a presentation as a group, you can all edit different portions of the presentation at once from various locations. This is much more efficient than the traditional route of having a long e-mail thread among team members using different file types.

THINGS TO KEEP IN MIND

- *Too much of a good thing.* Everything in moderation, right? When people first start using Prezi, they often get carried away. Too much zooming with too many paths (or slides) can be distracting and take the focus away from what you are trying to say. It can also make people dizzy, literally. So keep it simple. Limit your path count to around 40 to 50, and don't overdo the zoom.

- *Learning curve.* It can be intimidating to learn something new. If you take the time to look through all the great learning resources Prezi offers on its site and blog, you will see that it is a lot easier than it may seem at first.

- *Prezi isn't PowerPoint, and it isn't trying to be.* Prezi has differentiated itself by offering unique ways to deliver information, and with this comes some big differences. If you have been creating presentations for a while, there may be some elements such as animation, transitions, and favorite fonts that you are used to in other platforms that aren't in Prezi. But remember that Prezi offers a lot of new elements that will become your new favorites when designing presentations.

Prezi is an awesome brainstorming and designing tool for presenters. It is also a quickly evolving application that continues to incorporate feedback from users to deliver an optimal experience. It's what Big Fish used for our first client, and we haven't looked back since.

Emerging Tools

We love the existing presentation platforms, but we are always on the lookout for new ways to present. Let's take a look at a few emerging tools.

Bunkr is a simple platform that attempts to make presentation creation easier.[37] It uses many of the same features of other presentation platforms. Our favorite feature is that presentations are built on an HTML5 platform, meaning you can send a link to your presentation and it can be viewed on any browser on any computer, tablet, or smartphone.[38] We love this new focus because we understand that our world is going mobile. When you can display your presentations across all platforms, you are setting yourself up well for the future.

Projeqt was created by the global ad agency TBWA. Projeqt produces online presentations that can pull feeds from social networking sites such as Facebook, Twitter, and LinkedIn; RSS feeds; and many others. You are able to add real-time social networking updates to your presentation to provide an entirely new dimension to the experience. You can review audience feedback during the presentation and see how your talk is trending, all while on stage. This is just one of the great features of this platform, but features like this are going to change how the audience interacts with the presenter.

Kivo is an online tool that enables presenters to crowd-source feedback.[39] You upload your PowerPoint, and others are able to make annotations and comments on specific parts of your presentation. If you are collecting feedback from a large group of people, this is a great way to have it all in one place.

Slidedog allows users to seamlessly integrate many presentations and pieces of multimedia into one presentation experience.[40] There are times during an event or conference when you may have to switch files and programs, interrupting the presentation experience. This tool allows PowerPoint, Prezi, and videos to be integrated into one immersive experience.

And since we've talked about social media integration, there is also Tweetwall.[41] Tweetwall is an online tool that lets you customize and display trending tweets about your content. This allows you to engage directly with the audience and maybe even discuss some of your favorite tweets during the presentation. This tool and Projeqt are great ways to interact with your audience using social media.

Here are other favorites:

- Scrollmotion, an interactive mobile presentation tool that incorporates video elements; great for one-on-one meetings and managing sales team presentations

- Emaze, a website with 3D templates

- Haiku Deck/Haiku Deck Zuru, a tool that enables the speedy creation of design-centric presentations

- Sway, Microsoft's online presentation and website editor, with easily embedded interactive media

- Flowvella, an interactive slide presentation tool that can capture analytics

- Deckset, an instant content-to-deck simulator

- Slideklowd, a platform that shows real-time engagement levels during lessons

- VoiceBoard and similar platforms that are integrating Tony Stark–style presenting tools such as gesture and voice control[42]

Each of these companies is trying to provide solutions to many of the presentation problems we talk about in this book. They are all attempting to change how the world presents.

Draw It

Throughout this entire design chapter, we've made the assumption that you will be using a presentation tool to create your visuals. But there is another way.

Choosing to draw your visuals onstage is an awesome way to stay spontaneous. Drawing allows you to act creatively on the spot and gives you a sense of vulnerability that makes you more relatable. For example, instead of having slides animate an important process flow, draw it yourself. Take the audience through it in a more personal way. And by drawing it, you will be more likely to keep it simple and not overcomplicate the message. The act of drawing also focuses the audience's attention on you.

The three most common ways to do this are by using a whiteboard, pad of paper propped on an easel, or computer. One good example is Simon Sinek's TEDx talk, "How Great Leaders Inspire Action." He walks the audience through three questions that great leaders focus on to create change, and he illustrates each on a large piece of paper. The illustrations are simple. Using a marker, he shows these three important questions and the role they play in persuasion and action.

SIMON SINEK

"Start with Why"

Although this can be a great way to present, there are a few downsides to consider. Issues that can come up include scalability for larger presentations, the inability to use the whiteboard well, the need for data, and lack of visual diversity. By choosing this way to present, you are also adding another aspect for you to memorize during the presentation. Many new presenters who aren't totally confident in their speaking skills should be wary of this. Neophytes need to focus more closely on what they have to say and how they're going to stand up and deliver it.

Consider your message and your audience when deciding whether to draw, use slides, or forgo visuals entirely. What is the best way to engage the audience in your story?

Kenny's Tip

People ask me frequently what my favorite presentation tool is. I don't have a definitive answer, but I do have favorites, depending on the scenario. When I have to explain creative concepts, break down complicated material, map an area, create timelines, or brainstorm, I use Prezi. It works best with an audience that isn't conditioned to traditional methods (Prezi is commonly used at conferences such as TED). For a more word-heavy, corporate type of presentation (sales, investment, finance) that's fairly straightforward, I recommend sticking to PowerPoint and Keynote. These two platforms have presenter notes to help reduce the text. Also, in my TEDx talk, "The Art of Saying No," you'll note that I didn't use a presentation application. I spoke straight from the heart. Sometimes the best presentations are deck-free.

TIME CRUNCH

Your boss tells you that you need to make a presentation about your department's new initiative—and you have two hours to put it together. That sounds pretty stressful. We completely understand that a lot of the presentations that are given around the world are done under these conditions. We also realize that many of the tips that we have been giving about design and content may take a good bit of time to accomplish.

If you're pressed for time, we want you to concentrate on two things. The first is *focus on the message*. You don't have long, so you need to make sure that

you are choosing the best wording for each slide. This takes precedence over finding the prettiest and most relevant photo for the slide. People will remember the photo, but they will first look at what the slide is saying. When you're pressed for time, what matters is your message.

Second, *keep it simple*. Don't overthink your design, and do not overload your slides.

There are resources that allow presenters to create beautiful and engaging presentations from premade templates. The key here is that they are quick and easy to use. When you're in a last-minute situation, something that may not be fully customizable is OK. At this point, keeping information concise matters more than creating the most original slides.

Three platforms we recommend are Haiku Deck, Canva, and Deckset. These applications are available on the iPad, so you can create presentations on the go. Each has a web version as well. These resources have beautifully designed templates that allow presenters to create and share presentations when time is of the essence.

Kenny's Tip

While using templates for your deck enables you to prepare it quickly, some programs do not have the capability to customize transitions or slides according to your company brand guidelines. Sometimes all you need is a title slide, two to three content slides with your main points, and a closing slide. Don't create more than you need.

CONCLUSION

Some of what we've talked about will take you time to practice, but consider what the effort can mean for you in the future. If by making your information more visually pleasing and engaging for your audience, you will win more sales, convince your team of a change in strategy, or gain support for a new initiative, then it will all be worth it.

If you take one thing away from this chapter, we want it to be that design can make a difference.

Make your slides beautiful—not for the sake of aesthetics but for the sake of connecting. Connecting with the audience and delivering the message more clearly and effectively will drive a change in attitude and inspire action. Design for change.

As a presenter, remember that none of this matters if you cannot deliver it. If you craft a compelling story and design a beautiful deck, but you don't get up

there and present it well, all could be for naught. It's time to focus on how to deliver what you've designed.

Challenges

NOVICE

- Create a presentation with no more than five words to a slide.

- Design a deck with full-bleed photography.

- Create and deliver a presentation with a platform or application you have never used before.

EXPERT

- Deliver a 20-minute presentation while drawing all your points on a whiteboard.

- Conceptualize and create an infographic to explain a complex topic.

- Replace an important data set with an infographic.

DELIVERY

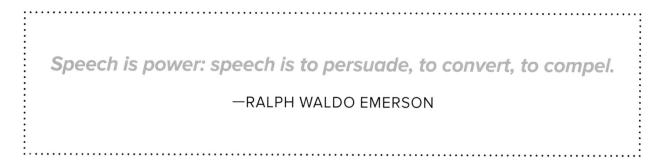

> *Speech is power: speech is to persuade, to convert, to compel.*
>
> —RALPH WALDO EMERSON

We've discussed the importance of great design, but what else makes a presentation worth not only watching but also remembering? Is it the topic? Yes. Is it the message? Yes. Is it how the presentation makes the audience feel? Yes. Do people walk away feeling they learned something? Do they want to tell their friends and co-workers about it? If they do, it's because the presentation was delivered to them in an emotional, impactful way. The presenter appealed to them, made them feel something, and instilled his message within them.

How?

Tone. Body language. Content.

These are the three elements that define a speaker's likability. Which one do you think is more important? You may be surprised to learn that most of what an audience likes about you doesn't have much to do with what you're saying but *how* you're saying it. Using cheerful, sincere facial expressions and a lighthearted tone is extremely effective in drawing interest in your presentation. While content is the most important element in any presentation, your delivery is key to your likability.

Think of content, design, and delivery as forces working in sync rather than in competition with each other. You can boost the memorability of your content with an incredible performance, and you can use beautiful design to give your delivery that extra "oomph." So what does excellent delivery actually mean?

In this chapter, we'll discuss the following:

- DISCOVER YOUR OWN DELIVERY STYLE

- TIME YOUR PRESENTATION

- BODY LANGUAGE

- CONTROL YOUR ENERGY

- THE POWER OF THE PAUSE

- GET RID OF VERBAL DISFLUENCIES

- CONQUER STAGE FRIGHT

- REHEARSAL

- EMERGENCY REHEARSAL

- WEBINARS

By the end of this chapter, we hope not only to give you a better understanding of presentation delivery but also to supply you with the tools you'll need to build and maintain the confidence of a seasoned presenter.

Don't have any issues with your delivery? Skim over this chapter for any extra tips and tricks, but if these topics sound too basic for you, then move on to Chapter 5, "Presenting an Experience," which is all about taking your presentation to the next level.

DISCOVER YOUR OWN DELIVERY STYLE

We're all unique individuals.

We form different opinions about the world. We each have our own ways of thinking, speaking, and moving. Our habits help define who we are as people.

We also have very different approaches to presenting information and communicating with an audience. Some believe presentations are meant to be purely entertaining, while others think providing the information as efficiently as possible is what matters most.

All great presenters are confident, optimistic, understanding, realistic, able, genuine, and engaging, but they display each characteristic in different ways. There's a great presenter inside all of us. Being able to

channel your skills is just a matter of finding your style and running with it. In this chapter, we'll help you determine your presentation style by playing to your strengths.

Before we jump into the different presentation styles, let's go over why it's important to establish your own.

One of the most powerful things you can be in a presentation is unique. That's why expressing yourself in an original way not only makes you stand out and maintain people's interest; it also sets you apart from other presenters and makes you more memorable.

You'll be a better presenter if you're comfortable with yourself. If you're not trying to mirror another presenter's style, your movements will be more natural and your voice will sound stronger and more confident. However, this isn't to say that you shouldn't pick up a few techniques from talented speakers. Having presentation role models is a great way to learn what you're capable of, but just mimicking them will undermine your authenticity.

Let's walk you through some delivery styles. As we cover each one, try to picture yourself physically giving a presentation using it. By the end of this section, you should have some idea of which style fits your personality and speaking abilities.

Keep in mind that these are broad categories. You might not necessarily belong to just one of these. You might have a combination of styles. You may find yourself drawn to a certain style but discover that another one is characterized by traits you exhibit. Experiment and see what works best for you.

Teacher

Do you like telling stories? Do you have the ability to captivate an audience with your words and demeanor? Even if it's just telling an old college story or recapping an episode of a TV show, the ability to tell a story compellingly is a gift and an indicator of being a teacher-style presenter. The teacher is a storyteller but is also skilled at listening to an audience, getting a feel for the room, and adjusting accordingly. *The teacher is able to make information relatable to the audience. Good teachers share complex information but make it simple, relevant, and meaningful.* If you have a natural tendency to inform your peers about certain subjects or delve deep in discussions, you just might be a teacher.

Examples: Simon Sinek, author and motivational speaker; David Rose, venture capitalist and entrepreneur; Seth Godin, author and marketer

Host

What does the host of a party do? Sure, hosts prepare the food, drinks, and music, and they create the general atmosphere of an event. But they also make you feel safe and comfortable; you trust and respect them. A good host, presentation-wise, is flexible, can read people, and builds credibility with them. Whereas a teacher is more apt to inform, a host wants to inspire an audience. As a host, you quickly make yourself relatable and create a comfortable, enjoyable environment for your audience. *A host reads the room and feeds off interactions. Whether it's through engaging audience members in activities, asking questions, or making people laugh, the host will emotionally connect with you and make you feel comfortable.*

Examples: Scott Harrison, founder and CEO of Charity: Water; Guy Kawasaki, motivational speaker and entrepreneur; Brené Brown, author and research professor

Coach

You don't have to give jaw-dropping locker room speeches to be a coach-style presenter. It entails being a leader and a thinker, meaning you inspire and motivate your audience. If you're naturally competitive and extremely passionate and not afraid to show it onstage, you're probably a coach. *Good coaches tend to approach tough topics with sensitivity, passion, and conviction and to feed that energy to the audience.* They make you stand up, cheer, and feel like you're able to do anything.

You're in the business of creating actual change. You want to see results. You might enjoy pumping up your friends or your team to do something big. If you're naturally competitive and extremely passionate, you're probably a coach. Now get out there and inspire your audience to action!

Examples: Jimmy Valvano, college basketball coach and professional broadcaster; Admiral William H. McRaven, ninth commander of U.S. Special Operations Command; Les Brown, motivational speaker and former politician

Headliner

Do you love the spotlight? Are you the life of the party? Are you the center of attention? You sound like a headliner. *As presenters, headliners tend to break down the wall by using language that's easy to understand, self-deprecating stories, and humor to warm up the crowd.* Headliners are good opening presenters; they get the audience in a good mood for the presenters who follow. Being a headliner in the presentation world is all about inspiring and delivering an entertaining message. You crave attention, but not in a negative way. You use your powers for good to lead your audience.

Examples: Steve Jobs, cofounder of Apple; Bill Clinton, former U.S. president; Maya Angelou, poet

Do any of these sound like you?

If you don't fall into one of these categories, do not be alarmed. These are simply starting points to help you develop your own style. People aren't just one type of presenter. We're all complex combinations. These four styles are offered here to give you a sense of direction.

If you have a sense of your presentation style, what do you do next?

Practice.

Now this doesn't necessarily have to be in the context of a traditional presentation. The best way to become more comfortable speaking in front of people is to actually do it, even if it's on a small scale.

For instance, the next time you tell one of your friends a story, practice speaking more clearly and work on the structure of the story. Gauge the person's reactions to see if you've made even a small impact. Doing this in social settings is great for your public speaking abilities. Over time, you will build up confidence in your style, whether you're a teacher, host, coach, or headliner.

Play off your strengths. You'll be more comfortable speaking if you know that you're naturally good at it. Combine that with practice and you will be one step closer to becoming a master presenter.

TIME YOUR PRESENTATION

Make sure you have finished speaking before your audience has finished listening.

—DOROTHY SARNOFF

Whether you have an hour or a month to prepare, you have a problem: you may have a lot to say but not enough time to say it.

Trying to cram all your points within a strict time frame, while juggling all the other elements involved in a presentation, can be a nightmarish situation. Stop stressing, and start reorganizing. If the foundation of your presentation is solid, it will show; your audience will be much more receptive to a strong, simple message than to a blur of information.

When it comes to writing a speech or presentation, it's important to remember that less is always more.

Respect your listeners. They're giving you two very important commodities that are scarce these days: attention and time. They didn't come because they want you to feel good about yourself. They came to be inspired. It's your job to make that happen.

No pressure, right? This is why it's important for you to connect with your audience quickly and effectively. Don't waste your and their time with unnecessary fluff. Cut the fat and get to the point without being impersonal. People won't mind that you're going straight to the core of your message as long as you're fulfilling their expectations. They'll actually appreciate the value you're placing on their time.

Let's say you have 25 minutes. Make your talk 15 minutes long. You have 45 minutes? Make it 35. You get it.

Why do you need to go under your time?

Because it forces you to condense your presentation and deliver the points that matter. It also allows time for you to recover in case you begin later than scheduled, go on an accidental tangent, or feel like a last-minute story or point would help improve the experience. Just make sure that you include and deliver every element your listeners expect so they don't feel that their time was wasted.

Break Apart Your Presentation

It's important to break your presentation into pieces. Each part must be honed and fine-tuned before they can come together to create a masterpiece. From the introduction and main points to the recap and closing, it's critical to practice and time each section individually. This lets you see which parts need to be shortened to make room for more critical points.

Estimate the Unknown

When you time yourself, prepare for all the elements beyond your talk: extra guest speakers, interactive

Whenever the issue of time comes up, think about your audience, not you and your information. We know from experience that it is a common problem many presenters face. Here are a few suggestions for effectively timing your presentation.

Know Your Time Limit and Go Under It

Always find out how long you have to present. Always. This will determine the amount of information you can include.

Kenny's Tip

Breaking apart your presentation will also help you "timestamp" parts of your presentation. For example, if your presentation is 45 minutes, you can break it down as follows:

- Opener: [3–5 minutes]
- Main Point One: [8–10 minutes]
- Main Point Two: [8–10 minutes]
- Main Point Three: [8–10 minutes]
- Recap of Topics: [2–5 minutes]
- Conclusion: [3–5 minutes]

Doing this enables you, during your presentation, to be mindful of where you should be and to adjust accordingly.

activities, video or product demonstrations, etc. This will help you keep things on track, but don't be afraid to cut something short if things get out of hand or go off-topic.

Have a Backup Plan

What happens when an audience member's question interrupts you? When your presentation is cut short? When you go over your time limit? These things happen, so it's important to adjust quickly.

A good example is when Kenny was forced to cut his speech "How to Turn Presentations into Experiences" at a large conference from 45 minutes to 30 minutes because the previous speaker had gone over time. Luckily, he was prepared because he had rehearsed the main points of his outline multiple times and was able to adapt while making light of the situation. As long as you communicate a central point, with supporting main ideas, you can always trim the fat from your presentation. Afterward, provide your audience with a way to follow up with you for more information. You can post the full slide deck to SlideShare with speaker notes so the audience can refer to it.

As long as you deliver information well, people won't be bothered if you end before your time is up. However, they'll be upset if you end late. Great talks pass quickly, and bad talks seem endless. The moment you begin speaking, you're on the clock and in danger of losing your audience's attention. The longer you go,

CONTROL YOUR ENERGY

Imagine you're listening to a very fast-speaking presenter. You're drawn by his energy and interested in his topic, and you're dying to learn more. Unfortunately, he's speaking too fast; you can't keep up.

Now reverse the scenario. You're listening to a slow speaker. The subject is fascinating, but her tone is putting you to sleep. She has no energy. You'd rather read this information online. How unfortunate.

You can avoid starring in these scenarios if you learn to *control your energy.*

This not only prevents you from becoming monotonous or overwhelming but also helps you become more effective at delivering your points. Watch speakers such as Steve Jobs and comedian Chris Rock. They know exactly how to control their energy to build suspense. They can balance passion with calm and dazzle their audiences for long periods of time. They are masters of themselves, which gives them the power to inform, persuade, or entertain whenever they choose. This is what separates a good speaker from a great one.

What's the secret to energy control? Well, there are actually three.

The first is *timing*. The moments when you choose to ramp up, slow down, pause for effect, and ask questions of the audience must correspond with your message. The best storytellers are charismatic and compelling, and they know how to calibrate their emotions as they tell the story. Having control over the timing of your actions directly affects how much control you have over your own energy throughout your presentation.

The second is *tone of voice*. Raising your tone when expressing excitement or lowering your tone when delivering important information prevents you from being, well, boring. After all, if you don't sound interested in your presentation, why should the audience be? Above all, the approach we recommend is one of balance. Balancing the ratio of excitement and calm is a good way not only to keep your audience engaged but also to keep yourself active.

The third secret is an ability that is truly rare: *empathy*. This is the ability to feel what people in the audience are feeling and adjust your speech according to their emotional demands. We know from previous discussion that knowing your audience is a fundamental concept in presentation delivery. Being able not only to identify with your listeners from a messaging

Kenny's Tip

Tone can be tricky, but it's one of my favorite elements to train people on because it can completely change the atmosphere of a presentation. Your intonation (the way your voice rises and falls when you speak, aka your pitch) is a very personal way to convey authenticity. Record yourself rehearsing a presentation and listen closely. Here are some things you should look for:

- You should sound confident, conversational, approachable, and not monotonous.

- Main statements should come off as calm, firm, and decisive.

- Are you speaking clearly enough? Are you out of breath? Are you too soft or too loud? Too fast or too slow? Do you put emphasis on certain words properly? Are you pacing yourself and pausing when needed?

- Listen for the rising of your voice at the end of your sentences. This should be reserved for questions, not statements. If delivering statements with a high tone at the end and not a firm tone throughout, you will risk sounding uncertain.

- Does the way you speak evoke the emotions you want the audience to feel?

standpoint but also to empathize with them from a delivery standpoint gives you the power to move them.

If you apply these three concepts successfully, you'll increase your chance of winning over your audience because they'll feel as though their needs were understood and met by you. Design your presentation to include specific points of interest as well as emotionally charged delivery; you'll be much more precise when trying to control your energy.

A great example is legendary basketball coach Jimmy Valvano's famous 1993 ESPY speech. Coach Valvano had terminal cancer, and many of his audience members were aware of and saddened by his diagnosis. Valvano understood this, empathized with his audience, and was able to move them.

How?

- *In his opener,* Valvano used humor and a lower tone to make his audience more comfortable. He carefully and expertly cracked a few jokes to ease the tension. This immediately helped to lighten the mood.

- *In his preview of topics,* he addressed his lack of cue cards; this was his way of letting the audience know that he was going to be authentic. From here, Valvano maintained a rising energy level to respond to the audience's energy. He raised his tone when emphasizing his three main points: laugh, think, and cry.

- *In his supporting content,* he described how he was "fired up" at his first coaching job. His tone matched his energy level and words. He also expressed humility and admiration, which is a great way to be relatable.

   Although Valvano's cancer diagnosis was grim, he made light of his situation by making fun of how he went over time in his speech but wasn't worried because he didn't have much time himself. He sprinkled his humor with a dash of reality.

- *In his conclusion,* Valvano used a somber tone. He listed the shocking cancer statistics and said how he believed people today could make a difference to help treat those like him. He was building tension before his big reveal.

- *For the climax of the presentation,* Valvano revealed his new foundation for cancer research, which resulted in the loudest ovation of the night. This is what happens when an audience's emotions are fully engaged throughout a presentation.

Cancer can take away all of my physical abilities. It cannot touch my mind, it cannot touch my heart, and it cannot touch my soul.

—JIMMY VALVANO

Legendary College Basketball Coach and Broadcaster

• *In his final statement,* Valvano slowly and firmly said, "Cancer can take away all of my physical abilities. It cannot touch my mind, it cannot touch my heart, and it cannot touch my soul." Then, in a humble gesture, he thanked the audience for their time.

We've learned from his presentation, and so can you. When delivering:

• sad news or statistics, use a somber tone.

• key points, show your excitement.

• a point you really want to stick, do it slowly.

• your final point, say it strongly, slowly, and confidently.

So How Do You Jump-Start an Audience's Energy?

If you see people looking away, checking their electronic devices, or even dozing off, it's going to be a battle to get them back. Empathize and respond accordingly.

Do an activity to get the audience engaged. This is, of course, based on the willingness of the audience, the crowd size, and the context of the presentation. You want to interact with the audience, but you don't want the activity to be irrelevant and unnecessary. If you've got a small crowd in front of you, feel free to get them on their feet and talking.

Nonverbal cues such as establishing and maintaining eye contact or walking past an audience member can pull people back into your presentation. A little movement can go a long way to nudge your audience and keep them on their toes.

If you begin to see people tuning out in the midst of a massive data dump, *tell a personal story* to get the audience's attention back. Humanize your data. Make it relatable and relevant to their lives. Adding a personal touch not only piques interest within the presentation; it also makes your information easier to remember afterward.

If your audience looks lost or in need of a breather, ask them to *stand up and stretch.* It will rekindle their energy and focus. You can also *ask questions midpresentation* to see if there are points that require further elucidation. Write down frequently asked questions and adjust your presentation to include the missing information next time. Taking the time to address any concerns is a great way to boost audience engagement as well as hone your delivery skills for the future.

Also, keep in mind that you're more likely to get an energetic audience in the morning. So if you have a choice of presentation time, request a morning slot to avoid late-day fatigue and after-lunch food comas.

When attempting to modulate your energy level properly in a speech or presentation, it's important to rehearse beforehand to ensure your points sync with your energy naturally. Energy is a powerful and scarce resource. Use it wisely.

Kenny's Tip

When I first started speaking, excessive movement onstage was my biggest tic. I learned to stand still, feet shoulder width apart, and to only move with purpose. Another challenge was adjusting my energy level to an audience whose first language was not mine. Speaking to people in a language that is not their native tongue can be a challenge when communicating important material. Overwhelming them with fast-paced delivery, distracting them with nervous movement on stage, and not speaking clearly can cause a complete disconnect. Pace yourself and observe your audience closely to see if they're following you. Adjust as necessary.

THE POWER OF THE PAUSE

We've all listened to a friend telling a story, a professor giving a lesson, or a professional delivering a speech in which information is flowing very fast. We've heard people stumbling over words just to fill the silence. In fact, we guarantee that you do this, too, many times without even realizing it. We'll discuss why you tend to use filler words and how to avoid this by deploying a powerful weapon that you already have in your arsenal. It's a very simple action you can take to dramatically alter the way you deliver your message, so take a deep breath and pause for effect. Literally. We're about to dive into the power of the pause.

First, let's talk about the problem.

They are called "filler words." We use them when we don't know what to say. We use them when we reach a gap in our thoughts and we feel pressure to fill that gap with anything, even useless phrases and incoherent babble. We want to maintain the rhythm of our speech, so we subconsciously resort to sputtering out whatever might cover our lack of direction. However, it does the opposite.

Instead of sounding smooth, we sound as though we have no idea what we're talking about. We seem disorganized and insecure, and the gap in our thoughts becomes obvious. But why? Why is it so hard to be silent between our thoughts? Why does there have to be a constant stream of sound when we present?

The root of the problem lies in our lack of patience. Most of us can't stand silence. It makes us uncomfortable. It isn't in our nature to pause in our speech. Also,

The right word may be effective, but no word was ever as effective as a rightly timed pause.

—MARK TWAIN

American Author

when we are eager to share something, our natural instinct is to rush. When we speak in front of people, we try to get our message across as quickly as possible.

You may think that pausing is a waste of time, so you try to fill that silence with other words. This isn't a terrible thing. You don't want to waste your audience's time; we get that. You want to be engaging and interesting, but if you're using filler words that add little value to your message, then you're actually wasting time without realizing it. Learning to pause in our thoughts *increases* our odds of finding the right word, phrase, or point. This is beneficial to your audience, who want those good, clear ideas that come from these pauses. Although we don't realize it, our listeners *crave* this silence. It gives them a chance to process the information, a chance to breathe.

Robert Byrd, a former U.S. senator and notable orator, once said, "There can be an art in the use of a pause. I find nothing wrong with a pause. It does not have to be filled with a *you know*. This phrase, like so many others, betrays a mind whose thoughts are often so disorganized as to be unutterable—a mind in neutral gear coupled to a tongue stuck in overdrive."

Slow down. Breathe. Think. Your audience will appreciate it, we promise.

When you're speaking in front of a crowd, your heart rate accelerates. It's because of this that every second seems like a minute. But if you can train yourself (and yes, it takes training) to pause a second longer than you can bear, you'll benefit as a speaker.

How?

Pausing between sentences helps your audience listen. They aren't trying to grab information as it whizzes by them. They want to absorb it at a reasonable speed. Let them digest your words at a natural pace and in comfortable chunks.

Good times to pause:

- When delivering and addressing the big idea of your presentation.

- When introducing and transitioning between main points.

- When explaining details that involve a large statistic. This can give the audience time to comprehend the data.

- When emphasizing points. Pauses can be a great way to underscore points and build emotion.

- After asking a question.

- When stating memorable lines of your presentation, such as your call to action. Exhale to relax and for greater impact.

Pauses also improve your demeanor as a speaker. You appear more confident when your message comes across in a direct, methodical manner. Ideas are stronger and more valuable when they aren't littered with irrelevant, meaningless babble.

The silence also allows you to breathe, which helps tremendously when speaking. It brings more oxygen to your brain, allowing you to focus on the right words. An extra breath also gives your voice more energy, which makes your words more attractive for your listeners. Breathing is such an important part of public speaking, and yet it is often dismissed as an obvious factor that doesn't require practice. However, being able to breathe effectively can take your presentation to the next level. Don't worry about appearing slow. Take a breath and let yourself think.

To master the art of the pause, you need practice and patience. An effective exercise involves reading a good piece of writing aloud slowly. Take your time and pause between phrases. Do this for at least a few paragraphs each day, and you'll begin to notice your heart rate decelerating and your words becoming clearer. It may feel strange at first, but it will pay off. For better results, pretend that you're in front of a crowd and try to glance at the page only a few times per paragraph. Read the paragraph over and over again, finding the phrases that belong together. This will help you work on your breathing and pausing technique at the same time.

Kenny's Tip

When delivering your main points, pause until the silence is almost unbearable. This is a powerful way to enable your audience to ponder and absorb the impact of your statement.

GET RID OF
VERBAL DISFLUENCIES

So, um . . . this book was, like, written 'cause, uh . . . you know . . .

Sound familiar? In the previous section, we talked about filler words and how to remedy them with a well-timed pause. Well, they're technically called verbal disfluencies. The formal definition of disfluency is the "impairment of the ability to produce smooth, fluent speech."[1] Most of us know what they are even if we don't know the technical term. These filler words and phrases pervade our conversations but usually go unnoticed.

Why do we use verbal disfluencies?

A major reason is that they serve as crutches in conversation, whether it's with your best friend or in front of hundreds of strangers. When you don't know what to say, you fill the silence with short, meaningless words or phrases. We have created our own defense mechanism against awkwardness. It happens on a subconscious level.

Even a phrase such as "I think" or "I believe" undermines the audience's confidence in the speaker and creates doubt. Imagine if Steve Jobs had said, "I think today Apple reinvents the iPhone," instead of, "Today Apple reinvents the iPhone." Notice the difference in impact.

It's important to be casual to a certain extent, but not sloppy. Being well spoken not only boosts your credibility but also makes your presentation much more enjoyable for your listeners, which causes them to be more attentive. People listen more carefully and respond more positively to those who are confident and smooth in their speech.

So how do we get rid of verbal disfluencies?

Know Your Content

The most effective and probably the easiest way to prevent verbal disfluencies is to know your content backward and forward. This is a highly underrated and very valuable piece of advice. It sounds obvious, but many overlook its importance.

Being prepared involves not only knowing what you're going to say but knowing as much as you can about the topic, too. It means knowing the ins and outs of the subject so well that you are flexible in your diction, not rigid—as you would be if you had memorized your speech.

An audience easily can tell if a presenter is regurgitating a memorized speech. And if you deviate from your script, you are more likely to fumble because you're bound to certain words and phrases. You'll be more likely to whip out an "um" or "you know" to fill that silence while you regain your train of thought. This, in turn, makes you seem unprepared and uncomfortable. Your confidence fades. Your rhythm is broken. You've lost your audience.

This can all be avoided if you know your information like the back of your hand. You can adjust to any error in your speech more quickly and smoothly if you've focused on mastering concepts instead of memorizing words. If you can answer most questions about the topic, you'll be nimble if distracted or interrupted. You'll be able to speak comfortably and consistently. And most important, you'll be able to weed out any verbal disfluencies.

Rehearse Your Presentation

Another method to do away with verbal disfluencies is to rehearse.

We mentioned that memorizing a script word for word is a bad thing, right? That doesn't mean you shouldn't have specific talking points or that you shouldn't practice your presentation extensively. Being well rehearsed is just as important as being well prepared, if not more so, when it comes to eliminating verbal disfluencies.

You don't know how things will sound when they come out of your mouth unless you actually practice saying them. If you trip on a word or phrase you thought would sound great in your presentation, you're naturally going to fall back on a verbal crutch. Trying to wing it is never a good idea.

So unless you're in a bind or you're forced to present at the last minute, you should always go over your entire talk at least three times before you present in front of an audience. Practicing for a presentation can be grueling, but it makes a world of difference to the audience when the presenter isn't constantly reaching for words while stumbling through an idea.

If you come across a phrase that does not flow naturally with the sentence structure in your speech, try speaking in short phrases rather than the long sentences you would read in a work of literature.

Use Silence

Another way to eliminate verbal disfluencies is by learning to harness the power of silence. As we speak, we naturally establish a rhythm that's made up of different inflections and speeds. When you become conscious of this, you're able to gauge when silence is necessary.

Kenny's Tip

Verbal disfluencies are bad habits. My biggest one was saying "you know" after a declarative statement. While it may seem minor, "you know" can make a person seem questionable and insincere (like a shady salesperson trying to convince someone).

In order to improve, I had a good buddy commit to making me do push-ups every time I said "you know" during a presentation or a normal conversation. Needless to say, my chest was pretty sore the first couple of weeks, but I eventually became more accustomed to letting myself pause instead of saying "you know."

Ask a trusted friend to keep you in check. Eventually you'll learn how to catch yourself. Push-ups aren't required, but they can be great negative reinforcement!

Silence is the best alternative to verbal disfluencies. "When in doubt, don't" is a good rule to live by. As noted earlier, there's nothing wrong with simply pausing. It allows you to catch your breath, organize your thoughts, and build anticipation for your audience. And it gives them time to digest your information. Pausing to breathe not only prevents you from using filler words but lowers your heart rate, which helps you stay calm and appear more confident.

You want to be natural and personable, but you don't want to dilute your message by using empty, unnecessary words. You want every sentence to mean something to ensure the greatest impact possible.

CONQUER STAGE FRIGHT

If you're like most people, then you've felt the fear that creeps up right before delivering a presentation. If this has occurred at least once in your life, relax. You are not alone.

According to the National Institute of Mental Health,[2] the fear of public speaking, which is called glossophobia, is the number one fear in America (that's right, over spiders, heights, and even death). A whopping 74 percent of Americans are said to suffer from this fear. Our anxiety about public speaking stems ultimately from the innate human concern with what others think of us.

Stage fright is absolutely normal. Even among the very best speakers.

To quote legendary comedian Jerry Lewis, "If you're not nervous, you're either a liar or a fool, but you're not a professional." Being nervous shows that you care about your presentation. It's how you handle it that separates a truly great communicator from a nervous wreck.

To show that we all have to start somewhere, here are a few well-known communicators who have had to overcome various speaking obstacles:

- *Winston Churchill (prime minister of the U.K.).* The English statesman battled a lisp, stammer, and strong case of stage fright throughout his career. He overcame speech impediments by tedious rehearsal and the development of his own eloquent speaking style during public addresses.[3]

- *Warren Buffett (investor).* After starting his business, the Oracle of Omaha enrolled in a Dale Carnegie public speaking course to calm his nerves. Once enrolled, he forced himself to stand up and talk to people by teaching a course at the University of Nebraska–Omaha.[4]

- *Richard Branson (entrepreneur).* Urged by his mentor, Sir Freddie Laker, to promote the Virgin brand himself, Branson rehearsed rigorously before giving public speeches to become more comfortable.[5]

- *Eleanor Roosevelt (First Lady and political activist).* Naturally shy, she improved by continually speaking in public in support of the campaign of her husband and thirty-second president, Franklin D. Roosevelt.[6]

- *Jay Leno (talk show host).* During his teenage years, Leno eased his nerves by performing his routine in an empty theater after his shift was over as a busboy at a local venue.[7]

- *Joel Osteen (minister).* Following in his father's footsteps as a preacher, Osteen preached every week, facing his fear of public speaking and constantly refining his craft.[8]

- *Louis C. K. (comedian).* He created rituals to calm his nerves that included sitting in silence backstage or taking a look at the crowd to get a feel of the audience.[9]

Every one of these people faced the exact same terrors that many of us do. They found a way to look beyond fear toward their goals. They didn't let their fear of speaking in front of others get in the way of their success.

While your stage fright may never truly go away, it's not the end of the world. The key is to find presentation rituals that you can customize and practice prior to stage time.

Here are a few:

- *Rehearse.* Practice constantly. Rehearse your presentation in parts to make it more manageable. Try to get feedback from a trusted group.

- *Laugh.* Scientific studies reveal that laughter creates a rush of endorphins (the feel-good hormone) to the brain, causing us to relax. Try listening to your favorite comedian's stand-up routines to calm your nerves before going on stage. Also learn how to laugh at yourself if you make a mistake while rehearsing or delivering your speech. You'll be able to recover more quickly and not give off negative energy.

- *Meditate.* Sit in silence and focus on the single most important idea you want your audience to take away from the presentation. Learning how to free your mind from distractions and controlling your fear can reap benefits beyond the stage (one of Kenny's favorite resources is reddit.com/r /meditation).

- *Feel the audience.* Take time to get to know audience members beforehand. Shake some hands and ask questions. You want to connect as much as possible.

- *Explore the venue.* If possible, check out the space. Rehearse your presentation on the actual stage and familiarize yourself with how you want to move through certain parts of your talk. This is one of Kenny's preferred methods.

- *Memorize your opener.* The most stressful part of a presentation is the first seven seconds. During this time, it's crucial to hook the audience. Memorize your opener to better ensure precise and concrete delivery.

- *Listen to music.* Listen to a song that calms you or pumps you up, depending on your preference. This is something Kenny does before going onstage.

- *Do breathing exercises.* If presentations give you anxiety, try some breathing exercises. Learning how to breathe properly helps you control your pace. A popular exercise that we recommend to our clients is to stand up, legs shoulder-width apart, with hands on your stomach, breathing in deeply and exhaling slowly.

- *Do visualization exercises.* Visualize your success on stage when rehearsing. What does the atmosphere feel like? What's going on in the background? How does the audience react to your presentation? For maximum effect, incorporate as many senses as you can into your visualization. You may combine this with meditation. This will boost your confidence prior to your speech; it will feel like you've already done this before.

Everyone has his or her own rituals to quiet stage fright. Don't be afraid to be creative as long as you find whatever works for you. Remember that the audience is rooting for you. They want you to succeed. No one is there to see you fall flat on your face. The audience is there for a good experience, and that happens only if you succeed. You're on the same side. Remembering that should help calm some nerves.

Ultimately, great communication is a habit.

REHEARSAL

We all know how important it is to rehearse your presentation. As with most things, a presentation requires a certain amount of preparation. However, preparing for a presentation is not the same as rehearsing it. When we talk about rehearsal, we mean the act of physically going through your entire presentation, and not just once but at least three times. Keep doing it

Kenny's Tip

I know I'm ready to deliver a presentation when I don't need a slide show to help me recall what to say.

until you feel comfortable and confident with your material and delivery.

It's just like playing an instrument. The more you practice, the better you get; and the better you get, the less nervous you'll be when you have to perform. Here are a few suggestions:

Time Yourself

The amount of time you have can shape the way you deliver your presentation. When you go over the structure, allot a specific, appropriate amount of time to each talking point. This not only helps you stay on track but allows you to adjust in the event of an interruption. Time yourself as if you were presenting in front of a crowd. Better yet, time yourself *while in front of a crowd.* You will be surprised by how much you will learn about yourself.

Consider other aspects of your presentation, such as your introduction by the host or a Q&A at its conclusion. Do you have 45 minutes to deliver your presentation? Finish in 35 minutes and leave enough time for a Q&A or more breathing room in case something goes wrong. It's always better to have too much time than not enough.

Get Feedback

It's important to understand what your strengths and weaknesses are. Ask a few friends, family members, or coworkers to critique your form. Ask what they felt was the best part of the presentation. Why? What could you have done better? Is there anything they didn't understand? Did they feel engaged and emotionally connected? The final, and most important, question should always be, "Did this presentation move you?" Make sure to tell those you are asking to be brutally honest with you. That is the most valuable feedback.

If you don't have the time to gather an audience, record yourself on your smartphone or video camera. Just as professional athletes watch films of themselves and their competitors to improve, so can you. This might be uncomfortable at first, but you'll be amazed by how much you will learn by watching yourself present. All the little things, from your voice projection to your hand gestures, become much more apparent when you can see yourself from the audience's perspective. Once you have an idea of what you're doing well and what you need to improve, you can build up your presentation skills. Whether you're getting real-time feedback from others in a small group or watching video of yourself, find a way to receive or do some form of critique. Trust us. It's worth it.

Kenny's Tip

When rehearsing, have your audience ask you as many questions as possible about your topic. This is an easy way to prepare for difficult questions. Come showtime, if you're asked a question you can't answer, don't fret. It's better to be honest and say you'll get back to them with the answer later. Just make sure you actually follow up through social media, e-mail, or another medium with the interested parties.

Rehearse in Real Time

Rehearse at "game speed" and don't stop until you feel like you've mastered every nook and cranny of your presentation. Every aspect should be rehearsed, from supporting content to slide design to verbal delivery. Practicing the specifics, right down to using the right inflection on a word or standing a certain way, will boost your comfort level on the day itself.

While you may want to rehearse in front of a mirror to get some visual feedback, you have to remember that this isn't how you're going to present in real time. You'll be looking at faces, some of which you will not recognize, and walking around on a stage with bright lights in your eyes. Go to the venue and play out your presentation. Your body will adjust to the environment, which frees up your mind to focus on the material.

———

What should you look out for when rehearsing (you may also use the points below as criteria when soliciting feedback)?

- *Body language.* Are you communicating confidence? How are your facial expressions, hand gestures, posture?

- *Timing of your presentation.* Are you staying within the time limit?

- *Tone.* How do you sound? Natural? Awkward?

- *Continuity of delivery.* Did you say anything that caused you to lose your flow?

- *Effectiveness of message.* Did you make the audience care? Did you use any jargon that may alienate your audience?

- *Timing of delivery.* Are you maintaining a good tempo? Are you breathing normally and not rushing through your presentation?

- *Comfort zone.* Do you feel anxious? Confident? Relaxed?

- *Audience response.* Did you develop a connection with your audience? Are you relatable?

You'll know you're ready when:

- You sound completely natural, and you can deliver your presentation without any awkward pauses or mispronunciations.

- All filler words are gone.

- Your delivery syncs with the slide transitions.

- You're able to present without any visuals.

- You would be excited to sit through this presentation yourself.

Everyone's different. We all have our own ways of practicing. No matter what unique rituals or methods you have, keep rehearsing. And continue to incorporate feedback and fine-tune your presentation until it's go-time. Keep at it until everything feels right.

But what if you don't have the time to rehearse?

Kenny's Tip

No presentation is perfect, so do not put that kind of pressure on yourself. There will be factors that are out of your control. It's all about mastering your presentation to the point where you can adapt to any situation.

EMERGENCY REHEARSAL

Not everything goes as planned. And that's OK.

We want you to be prepared for the unexpected moments that are bound to happen at some point when you're presenting. Whether you forget you have to give one in the first place or you're forced into an impromptu presentation, we're here to provide you with a few tips on rehearsing under pressure.

If, for some reason, you have very limited time to rehearse, don't worry about the details. First things first: nail down the content. Focus on your main idea. Can you summarize your message in a single sentence? If not, work on narrowing it down. The content is the foundation of your presentation. It's why you are presenting, so make sure you have a firm grasp of it. The sooner you can home in on your central message, the more time you have to rehearse the next most important aspect: delivery.

People will always remember the presenter more than the presentation. If you have only a little time to rehearse, make it count. Don't get caught up in unnecessary details. Go over the structure you created and practice your points until they sound completely natural. You can even use the situation to your advantage. By making light of the circumstances and being transparent, you have something you can talk about, even if it's making fun of yourself. Your audience will see that you're relaxed and will appreciate your candor. Once you feel comfortable with what you're saying and how you're saying it, use the remaining time to simplify whatever visuals you may have on hand.

Odds are that you won't be required to showcase a professionally designed deck, but if you have extra time, prepare a few slides that are clean and aesthetically pleasing.

Early in Big Fish's history, Kenny was asked to deliver an impromptu 15-minute presentation to a roomful of startup entrepreneurs. The catch? He had only an hour to prepare. No copywriters, no designers, nothing.

So what did he do? Well, to start, he focused on two things: getting to know the audience members and connecting emotionally with them. He broke his preparation time into 30 minutes of content creation and 30 minutes of section rehearsal.

Next step, he identified a big idea. Then he quickly structured his speech into three parts: an opener, supporting content (three facets of the big idea), and a conclusion that included a call to action.

An audience is more likely to remember information presented in three parts. Kenny followed the "rule of threes" and crafted three important points he wanted the audience to take away, and then he layered supporting content for each of the points. This made it not only easy to remember but also easy to follow. He finished with a section that recapped his main points.

When he was done, his structure looked like this:

- Opener

- Main point 1

- Main point 2

- Main point 3

- Recap of points

- Closing/call to action

After this, he focused on creating a powerful opener. How? By starting off with a personal story that allowed the audience to get to know him and establish a bond. Kenny then discussed the main points, which set up a call to action that was simple yet effective. In this case, he chose to end with a quote reflecting on the impact of presentations and a question challenging the audience to step up their presentation game.

His structure now looked like this:

- Opener *(Story of Big Fish Presentations.)*

- Main point 1: Storytelling *(What are the elements of a good story? Context, hero and villain, suspense.)*

- Main point 2: Design *(What are the principles of good design? Tell, instead of show, as there was no time to prepare a slide deck. Make the audience laugh at the irony.)*

- Main point 3: Delivery (*How body language, passion, and tone can impact your audience.*)

- Recap of points (*Storytelling + Design + Delivery = Experience for the Audience.*)

- Closing/call to action (*Quote and questions.*)

Kenny's Tip

I did not have time to create slides for this presentation. I'd rather have no slides than bad slides. Focusing the majority of my time on the delivery and content resulted in my landing a couple of new accounts. If you find yourself pressed for time, here are three quick tips:

1. Leave the slides for last. Spend your time crafting a clear message. What does your audience want or expect?

2. Do not fret over the script. A bulleted outline will do, and you can transcribe your presentation later using apps such as Dragon Dictation.

3. Save enough time for at least one run-through and record it so you can watch and refine parts of the presentation where you don't feel comfortable.

After Kenny created the content, he focused on delivery. Once he felt he had each section rehearsed, he timed a full run-through. He continued to edit content until showtime. Despite the time constraints, Kenny did well, and the presentation was warmly received.

He established an emotional connection with his audience through storytelling and self-deprecating humor. Meeting a few audience members before the presentation also helped.

If you have to give an impromptu presentation, keep in mind that people will always remember you more than the presentation. Make sure you appeal to the heart more than to the brain.

We think it's appropriate to close this section the same way Kenny closed his presentation. You're probably still wondering what quote he ended up using, right?

People may not remember exactly what you did, or what you said, but they will always remember how you made them feel.

—Maya Angelou

WEBINARS

We live in a digital world, and so it is not surprising that we are frequently asked how to give good presentations through nonpersonal, digital formats such as webinars that take place remotely and online. While you may not have to worry about stage fright when giving a webinar, that can be a double-edged sword. How do you connect with an audience that's not physically in front of you?

- *Create a calendar.* Create a schedule that outlines what you need to accomplish before the day itself: creating content, completing slides, doing a full rehearsal, promoting the webinar, testing the AV equipment, engaging with attendees, and so on. Webinars can be more time-consuming than an onstage presentation.

- *Check the AV equipment.* Make sure you have a stable WiFi connection, a good microphone or headset, and reliable web conferencing programs (such as Go-to-Webinar or Webex) before you even begin marketing your webinar. Test these constantly to make sure you're ready.

- *Give your webinar a catchy title.* A good, relevant headline is vital to compel the audience to sign up and tune in. Just make sure the topic is of interest to your target audience.

- *Consider a panel of multiple speakers.* Having only one speaker can be monotonous. Consider featuring multiple speakers to change the pace of the webinar and keep the audience interested. Just make sure each panelist speaks to a different aspect of your subject to prevent redundancy. Have your additional speakers market the event to their networks.

- *Market your presentation.* Share your event with your contact list, blog subscribers, and social media friends and followers. For their convenience, create a message template for them to share with their friends. Here's a brief example:

  > Hey (person's name)! Here's a cool webinar that's coming up on (date, time, location) by (your name) of (your company). He's really good at (subject), and I believe it will help you grow (the recipient's company) by (the bullet point version of the content of the webinar).

  > Don't market it too far in advance. We recommend two to three weeks prior to keep it fresh in your attendees' minds. If you want to go the extra mile, send attendees a handwritten note or marketing collateral.

- *Send reminders.* Treat your webinar like an event. Send a friendly calendar reminder at least two weeks prior, so attendees can sort out their schedules. Provide a date, time, and easy ways to share the webinar details with their networks, along with instructions on how best to tune in. If they have to download any software or extensions beforehand, tell them. It is also good practice to reach out and remind your attendees an hour before the event to confirm that it is still on.

- *Keep the webinar short and sweet.* Fifteen minutes may be too short, but over an hour is too long. You're asking participants to give you their undivided attention and promising them value. The sweet spot is between 30 and 45 minutes, with 10 to 15 minutes reserved for Q&A. You are competing with many other distractions for your viewers' attention.

- *Deliver unique or original content.* Webinars must have a focused subject with material that cannot easily be found online. If you can pull the same information from a Google search, share that instead of presenting for an hour. Never waste your audience's time.

- *Present your slides slowly.* Going through your slides too quickly can be distracting for a viewer. Slow down. Your main focus should be to engage the audience with your content. If you have a large number of slides, give your audience a way to access the deck after your presentation. Post it online and share it socially.

- *Encourage audience interaction.* During the webinar, encourage the audience to e-mail you, send you questions, or tweet you with a unique hashtag (this can build more social traction for you, too). Make sure you have someone feeding you the questions and helping you respond if it's a larger audience. It can be tough to maintain attention spans online *and* communicate through social platforms.

- *Avoid background noise.* If you have a formal, scripted pitch, mute your attendees and ask them to send you questions through the social network you're using for the webinar. Having too many people talking at once—or having background noise—can be very distracting.

- *Provide actionable advice.* Like any presentation, webinars should have actionable advice that attendees can use. It's good practice to share materials online right after your webinar so attendees can learn more or reach out to you.

- *Reuse your content.* Record the webinar and upload it on websites such as your blog, YouTube, and SlideShare. Share it as quickly as possible so it's still fresh in the minds of your audience.

Webinars can be great for marketing purposes, internal conference calls, or workshops. Remember, just because you're not there physically doesn't mean that you get a free pass. It's still up to you to manage your audience's attention.

Give people a reason to listen, and you will succeed.

CONCLUSION

The art of presentation delivery involves connecting with your audience, maintaining their interest, and making yourself memorable. Giving a presentation in a confident, passionate, and entertaining way is always a challenge. You have to discover your own delivery style, get the timing just right, use body language effectively, get rid of verbal disfluencies, and rehearse tirelessly. But if you get it right, the audience will remember it, revisit that memory, and share it with others.

This is how change happens.

In the next chapter, we'll talk about the importance of and how to create the overall presentation atmosphere. Giving a presentation is not only about delivering a message, it's about delivering it in a unique, memorable way that can change the audience's hearts and minds. It's about presenting an experience.

Challenges

NOVICE

- Experiment with a new ritual before your next presentation.
- Give your next presentation with five to seven minutes to spare while hitting all your necessary points.
- Record yourself rehearsing and note your verbal disfluencies, body language, and energy level.

EXPERT

- Give a presentation with no more than three verbal disfluencies.
- Schedule a rehearsal with a live audience and use the questions in the "Get Feedback" section.
- Deliver a 20-minute presentation without a slide deck.

PRESENTING AN EXPERIENCE

Nothing ever becomes real till it is experienced.

—JOHN KEATS

How would you define an experience?

Is it the physical space around you? Is it the sights, sounds, and smells that you take in and remember? Is it the people you're with? Or is it something more?

When we say we believe in creating an experience, we're talking about the feeling people get when an idea resonates with them.

When you share your ideas with an audience, your goal isn't simply to give them a set of talking points. A piece of paper can do that. You're not there just to show them pretty pictures and ramble on so you can hear your own voice. A great presentation is meant to inspire, entertain, or persuade an audience to create change.

We've discussed design, content, and delivery, but this chapter is going to be a little different. We'll give you tips on how to be an even better presenter, but our main goal is to instill within you the desire to go above and beyond your presentation. Look beyond the slides and the stage and think about what you're going to leave with your audience.

In this chapter, we'll discuss the following:

- STAND OUT
- PRIOR TO THE EXPERIENCE
- INVOLVE THE AUDIENCE

- AFTER THE EXPERIENCE
- HOW TO GET VALUABLE FEEDBACK

As you write, design, and practice your presentation, think about the memory you want to create for the people to whom you're speaking. Do you want them merely to nod along, write things down, and tell their friends? Or do you want them to feel something unique, something that stays with them for years?

If you'd like to do the latter, you're ready to dive into presenting an experience, the culmination of the Big Fish process.

STAND OUT

It's one thing to give a great presentation. It's quite another to create a unique, exciting, and memorable experience. Sure, it may be easy to give a 30-minute presentation where you show some good-looking slides and share some pretty interesting ideas. There's nothing wrong with that. It gets the job done.

But what if you could do more? What if you could make a lasting impression on your listeners? What if you could craft an experience that leaves them in deep thought on their way home, changes how they see an issue, or, even better, actually makes a difference in the world?

To truly make an impact, use the three steps of the Big Fish process to turn your presentation into an experience for the audience:

- Engaging content

- Memorable and simple visuals

- Powerful delivery

Engaging Content

First rule: know your content. Second rule? Know your content so well that you can share it through a story. Telling a structured story gives your presentation the exciting edge that keeps audiences hooked. Plan what you're going to say in extreme detail. You may think that just by knowing the content you'll be able to wing it out there. You certainly might be able to, but you won't stand out. Your audience will pick up on the tiny things, like reaching for a word or going off on a tangent. When your listeners notice these, they'll most likely lose respect for you subconsciously. Having a solid road map of your presentation will give you extra confidence your audience will not only notice but also remember.

Memorable and Simple Visuals

When you are crafting your presentation, your slides should be an aid to the experience and never a crutch for your lack of preparation. Every slide should have a strong message with minimal text and a unique design. Create visuals that complement your information and do not distract your audience. Too many images or words on a screen are difficult to digest and even tougher to remember. Instead of cluttering a slide, break the content down and spread it across several slides. Your audience will remember quick phrases, simple images, and short videos. Incorporating bold design into a strong message makes you an unforgettable and unique presenter.

Powerful Delivery

Tone. Body language. Passion. These aren't pertinent to your content or design, but they are extremely critical to delivering an experience. You could have an interesting topic backed by a beautiful slide deck, but if you ramble on in a disorganized way, it won't matter.

Your presentation will fall flat. Always rehearse your presentation over and over and over again. Your content might be structured, but actually saying the right words that reflect your content takes practice. A well-rehearsed delivery can turn an OK presentation into a stellar one. Once you're comfortable with verbalizing your content, focus on expressing your thoughts passionately to make yourself a memorable speaker.

———

If you've mastered these three steps, you'll give a memorable presentation. But let's challenge ourselves. If you really want your big idea to be heard, forge a way to connect with your audience.

Using the Five Senses

Appeal to the five human senses. Think of each sense as a channel by which to reach your audience. Presentations normally invoke only sight and sound, but what if you go beyond that? Don't miss out on some unique opportunities to be different. Here's how you can tap your audience's five senses.

SIGHT

Incorporate something unusual, such as a dazzling technology demonstration or a magic trick that fools the audience. Techno-illusionist Marco Tempest does both using elaborate digital props, advanced lighting, and good old-fashioned showmanship. Seeing is believing, after all, and anything that challenges an audience's beliefs can be compelling if delivered in the right way.

TASTE

When Kenny was in sixth grade, his reading class was learning about Vietnamese culture. Kenny's mother came and spoke about her journey from Vietnam to America and how she learned to make various dishes to support her family. During her talk, students were given spring rolls (a traditional Vietnamese dish) and shown what goes into making them. All their senses were engaged: the crunch, smell, feel, sight, and taste of the roll.

Logistically, it might be tough to feed an entire audience, but when showcasing a product that is consumable, it's a good way for your audience to truly understand what you're selling.

Kenny's Tip

For a video recipe of my mother's delicious spring rolls, visit http://www.flipmyfood.com/segment/grilled-pork-spring-rolls.

In Jinsop Lee's TED talk, "Design for All Senses," Lee advocates utilizing design to create more memorable, extrasensory experiences. He closed his talk by throwing candy to the audience. Don't try this at a dental conference!

TOUCH

Incorporating touch into your presentation allows audience members to experience something directly, whether you're demonstrating a new piece of technology or trying to prove a bigger point. Remember how cool it was in grade school when your science teacher talked about fossils and passed around samples for you to touch? You could feel the weight of the fossils in your hands and imagine what the plants and

Kenny's Tip

One way to create an immersive experience is by incorporating 3D printing into your presentation. This works for companies looking to create small prototypes of their products in pitches. Sending a design to the Maker Bot store will give you an edge when pitching to an audience that needs to see a physical and tangible product. For free 3D models, go to http://www.123dapp.com/.

animals must have been like alive. This made the experience and message even more intimate. It was cool then, and it's even cooler now.

SMELL

Smell can be very risky if not done right, but incorporating scents into your presentation is a powerful way of letting the audience become part of your story. Whether it's sharing the aroma of food when talking about your mother's cooking or spraying the awful cologne you wore to tell the story of an awkward first date, scent can be a powerful ally or your biggest enemy. Just enough of it can set the scene for your story, but too much of it can be distracting. Use at your own risk.

SOUND

Take advantage of sound in your presentations, from playing pieces of music to altering the way you speak. As long as sound is relevant, it is always better to show, not tell. If you're talking about sound waves or early jazz, your audience will be much more involved and interested if they can hear some examples. For example, in his TED talk, "The Transformative Power of Classical Music," Benjamin Zander played the piano to illustrate his point. Instead of merely explaining the power of storytelling behind the music, he actually showed us. You can enhance the effectiveness of your presentation significantly by incorporating sound into your message.

The goal of triggering each sense is to evoke an emotional response in your listeners and keep them engaged. Just make sure the venue can handle whatever you're planning.

You won't always have a chance at reconnaissance, but if you're able to do a walk-through, you definitely should scope out the place. Even if you're not planning on using holograms, advanced robotics, or backup dancers, try to get a feel for the environment in which you'll be presenting. Like a tactician on a battlefield, knowing the landscape will only increase your chances of victory. Walk around, ask questions, practice your delivery, check power outlets, and tap on microphones.

When thinking of ways to blow your audience away, make sure you can actually execute your ideas. Rehearse everything in real time to ensure success on presentation day.

Examples of Creative Presentations

If you're looking for inspiration, watch presentations given by the pros. One great resource is TED. Organizations such as TED focus on making their conferences an emotional and memorable learning experience for the audience. By watching some of the best speakers give unforgettable presentations, you'll not only become inspired, you can also try to incorporate some of their techniques in your next presentation.

Here are some examples of presentations that use simple but powerful delivery techniques to create memorable moments for the audience.

USING STATISTICS

In his TED talk, "Teach Every Child About Food," chef Jamie Oliver stated, "Sadly, in the next 18 minutes when I do our chat, four Americans that are alive will be dead from the food that they eat."

Open with a shocking and relevant statistic that communicates the urgency and importance of your presentation.

USING STORY

In "The Danger of a Single Story," author Chimamanda Ngozi Adichie shared how the power of stories enabled her to find her unique voice in her work.

Use engaging and personal stories to connect emotionally with and motivate your audience.

USING DESIGN

In David Epstein's talk, "Are Athletes Really Getting Faster, Better, Stronger?" he uses bold slide design to show how physical feats have evolved over the years.

Use high-quality slides that require little to no explanation to emphasize your point.

USING A THOUGHT ROAD MAP

In his 2014 commencement address to the University of Texas at Austin, Admiral William H. McRaven identified and elaborated on 10 different takeaways from Navy SEAL training.

Preview the number of points at the beginning of your presentation to give your listeners a mental road map of where they are in the speech.

USING SUSPENSE

In his iPhone announcement keynote, Steve Jobs talked about the capabilities of three products before introducing a revolutionary product that would combine all three.

Build on your points for a grand reveal of the big idea.

USING SHOCK

In his TED talk, "Mosquitos, Malaria, Education," Bill Gates released mosquitos into the room to evoke the discomfort the audience should feel at learning the frightening truth about malaria.

ERIK WAHL

E-Biz Forum 2012

flickr/IDEA4Industry

Do something out of the ordinary to illustrate your point, and dare to make the audience uncomfortable if it serves your message.

USING PROPS

We interviewed TEDx speaker Dima Ghawi, who talked about breaking out of her cultural limitations and discovering the leader within. In her TEDx talk, "Breaking Glass: A Leadership Story," Ghawi spoke of how her grandmother compared a Middle Eastern girl's reputation to a glass vase. If cracked or broken, it would always be seen that way. Later in life, Ghawi broke out of the imaginary glass vase of constraints. At the end of her TEDx talk, Dima broke an actual vase onstage and gave each member of the audience small pieces of it, wrapped with the message "Remember to break through your limitations." This helped the audience stay connected with her story long after the event.

Use props or physical objects to illustrate your main points or call to action.

USING ART

Graffiti artist Erik Wahl live-paints as he tells his story.

You can show firsthand the process of creating art or tell a story through painting or drawing. Watching a piece unfold before your eyes can be captivating for an audience.

USING VIDEO

During a presentation at Google I/O 2012, the Google cofounders videoconferenced with an in-air skydiver wearing Google Glass (an augmented reality device that has a capability to show others what you are seeing). For dramatic effect, the skydiver landed in the venue and joined the crowd.

Use video with emotionally resonant content to showcase how your product or service can change the lives of others.

USING HUMOR

Comedian Maysoon Zayid performed a TED talk called "I Got 99 Problems . . . Palsy Is Just One." Zayid told her story of living with cerebral palsy with self-deprecating humor, charm, and wit, and the audience couldn't help but fall in love with her. She used incredibly personal material that kept the audience hooked and laughing the entire time.

USING MATH

In "A Performance of 'Mathemagic,'" Arthur Benjamin shows how he can mentally compute intricate math problems simultaneously with a calculator.

Showing off amazing or complex skills is awe-inspiring and gets people thinking.

USING MUSIC

Benjamin Zander played live music in his TED presentation, "The Transformative Power of Classical Music."

Playing music isn't just a way to entertain your audience; it is also a perfect way to show rather than tell.

USING DANCE

"Dance vs. PowerPoint, a Modest Proposal" is a pathbreaking TED talk created through a unique collaboration among writer John Bohannon, choreographer and director Carl Flink, and his dance company, Black Label Movement, that used dancers instead of a PowerPoint deck to illustrate the presentation.

USING MAGIC

Keith Barry puts on an incredible magic show with audience members in "Brain Magic."

Magic is a classic form of entertainment that can be used to make a point that will really stick with an audience.

USING SCIENCE

At the World Science Festival, Bobby McFerrin showed the audience how our brains are wired to the pentatonic scale. Locations onstage corresponded to certain notes. As he moved around the stage, the audience responded with the appropriate notes on the scale. By doing so, McFerrin effectively played the audience as a musical instrument. The result was astounding, and the audience loved it. You can watch McFerrin's presentation on the TED website under "Bobby McFerrin Demonstrates the Power of the Pentatonic Scale."

———

Try not to do too much. You don't always have to give a TED-like performance every time you present, but it's important to allow yourself to be truly creative. Express yourself and give your audience a window into your passions. Doing something unique always makes for a memorable experience.

If what you already have drives the point home, that's fine. If you aren't accomplishing anything significant by incorporating additional elements into your presentation, then don't include them. Ultimately, what matters is that the audience understands your message and acts on it.

JOHN BOHANNON

"Dance vs. Powepoint, A Modest Proposal"

BOBBY MCFERRIN

World Science Festival

haak78/Shutterstock.com

PRIOR TO THE EXPERIENCE

As you already know, crafting a great presentation requires preparation. You want to make sure that all the pieces work together and that everything goes according to plan. What else can you do?

Get your name and your message out to the world. Establish and maintain an engaging social media presence. Promoting yourself in the right way can increase your audience size and expand your network.

Create a catchy title for your presentation that is easily shareable, straightforward, and engaging. Make it something worth opening and sharing. Give people a solution to a problem. Pique their curiosity. Appeal to their interests. However, be mindful of the frequency of your promotion. You want your potential listeners to be aware of your presentation, but you don't want to exhaust them with repeated messages.

The same goes for how early or late you begin that dialogue with your audience. You want to find a happy medium between early enough to give people time to plan on coming but not so far in advance that they forget about the event closer to the date.

Kenny's Tip

When I have a speaking engagement, my team normally starts promoting between two to three weeks before the event. This allows me to connect on social media with any attendees prior to the presentation who can tell me what they expect to hear. I've done this and hung out with attendees before my speech, and I've created some incredible bonds. Not only is this awesome, but on the day itself, there is nothing like having a few fans in the audience.

Promote your presentation through your website, social media channels, and news outlets that can reach interested attendees. Treat your presentation like a campaign and market it to influential individuals who can attend and bring their friends. It never hurts to speak to your event coordinator about how he or she plans to promote the event so you can determine if there are joint marketing opportunities. For example, for TEDxLSU, the marketing team released the names of a small number of speakers. When Kenny's name was announced, Big Fish Presentations shared videos previewing the talk in social media posts.

Other ways to build buzz:

- Collaborate with the event organizer on ways you can promote your speech by utilizing the conference channels. If the organization has a blog or newsletter, contribute an article so all attendees can read it. The organizer also may have special hashtags on Twitter for you to connect with the conference audience.

- Invite potential prospects, customers, or investors to your event, offering them free advice that they would otherwise have to pay for (just make sure you deliver).

- Use Facebook, Twitter, and LinkedIn to research and connect with your audience.

- Provide a small part of your presentation (using SlideShare) to prep your audience for the upcoming material. This helps boost goodwill and credibility by giving away something of value. Make sure not to give everything away, though.

- Find out which journalists or bloggers are attending your session and offer to do interviews afterward.

- When marketing your talk to attendees, offer a giveaway or prize for correct answers to questions you may ask.

- Hire a professional to record your presentation, so you can upload it to social media afterward.

Kenny's Tip

While this specific section is geared more toward conference speaking, these lessons also apply to smaller-scale presentations. If I'm delivering an internal presentation to the members of my team, I send an agenda so they know what to expect. That way, they can prepare questions and even submit them to me beforehand.

INVOLVE THE AUDIENCE

One of the basic principles of public speaking is audience interaction or audience engagement. You should always be speaking *to* the people in your audience, not *at* them. This is a great philosophy to live by. However, if you want to truly engage with a group of people, what better way than to get them involved in the presentation?

Many, even the best presenters, get trapped in a "presentation bubble" of sorts. We get caught up in our thoughts and forget to cater to our audience in real time. You might be so focused on hitting the right points, enunciating clearly, and making eye contact that you neglect to interact with the human beings in front of you. It's something that is so easily and often forgotten that audience members have become accustomed to a standard presentation. A speaker appears on stage, maybe asks a question, and walks around a little bit. In a way, this can be beneficial for you as an up-and-coming presentation star. If audience members are used to seeing the same old presentation, then anything even remotely different or exciting will be leaps and bounds better than any other presentation they've seen.

John Medina, researcher and author of *Brain Rules*, says that the brain begins to tune things out after an average of 9 minutes and 59 seconds no matter how interesting the subject. During this time, it's imperative that you start providing engaging avenues where your listeners can reconnect not only with you but also with each other.

It's all about closing the gap between audience and speaker and creating an experience that everyone can share, even for a few minutes.

There are many different types of presentation settings and situations, from small boardroom events to colossal global summits. Of course, each type has its own potential for audience interaction, but here are a few tactics that can apply to many.

Activities

Prompting the audience to participate in an activity is probably the most effective way to induce engagement. Activities compel the audience to perform an action instead of just listening. When they are given a task or prompted to think for themselves, they feel as if they are contributing. Therefore, they have a stake in your presentation. You have given them a sense of purpose and direction.

Remember Erik Wahl, the graffiti artist? He asked audience members to demonstrate bravery by performing various embarrassing activities. In return, he gave away works of art that he painted during his presentation. Everyone wanted one, and Wahl knew that. He kept them engaged by creating suspense and by putting something at stake.

The activities you choose can range from simple ice-breakers to single-player or multiplayer games. They should get the audience to compete, work together, or simply have fun. It doesn't necessarily have to relate directly to your message, but it certainly helps if it does. Your goal is to get people's blood flowing, mouths talking, and minds working. You want your listeners to be alert, ready to receive your message.

For smaller groups of 15 to 25 people, a good ice-breaker with which to open workshops and assess the audience's knowledge is the alcohol-free version of "Never have I ever." Have all attendees hold up 10 fingers, begin with "Never have I ever," and finish with a statement like "read off every single slide in a presentation." When an audience member is guilty of the statement, he or she puts a finger down. Keep this going until there are no fingers up or you run out of questions. Depending on the competitive nature of the audience (sales teams and execs are particularly competitive), you might throw in a prize, such as a gift card. Besides creating conversation, this is a fun and easy way to present points or facts that may raise awareness about a cause.

Other activities:

- *For small audiences.* Break into groups to discuss a challenge and share the results with the room.

- *For larger audiences.* Role-play processes, such as a sales interaction, with an audience member.

- *For audiences of all sizes.* Quiz the audience and reward participation with a prize.

Kenny's Tip

Finding memorable ways to get the audience to laugh at themselves makes you more likable and accessible. One of my favorite things to do in my keynotes is to get a volunteer from the audience to model what I describe to be good body language. For example, if I say, "Make eye contact," the volunteer often stares at the crowd in a creepy, yet humorous, fashion. It's a great way to break the ice.

Questions

Questions go beyond just asking people in the audience to raise their hands or clap in response. Get creative. For example, with groups in which participation is welcomed and encouraged, you can use a tool such as Catchbox (http://us.getcatchbox.com/). The person who catches the box has to say what he or she is most curious about with regard to your subject.

In addition to the postpresentation Q&A, it's good o keep the audience on their toes by asking them questions that relate to your topic. If you're trying to introduce a new concept, you may use an audience member as a real-life example or get real-time feedback about something you just said or did. People will be more accepting of an idea if it is being tested or applied right in front of them. Be transparent. If an idea isn't working, show that you're flexible. Be aware that asking questions of your audience means you have to be prepared for anything. Anticipating questions makes you a stronger presenter, and being natural with your answers builds credibility that sticks with people.

QUESTION ETIQUETTE

- You may field questions midpresentation.

- If you don't know the answer to a question, admit your ignorance. It's even OK to ask if an audience member knows the answer. This can reengage the entire room's attention. If no one knows, make sure you actually follow up through e-mail or social media with the answer.

- Stay silent after asking a question. This will compel someone to volunteer an answer.

- In response to questions, answer with something along the lines of "Thank you for your question" instead of "Great question!" You don't want to sound sarcastic or patronizing.

We recommend recording all the frequently asked questions in your presentations so you can prepare good answers.

Live Demo

Getting an audience member to demo a product live accomplishes multiple goals: it involves the audience in your presentation, it captures interest and builds suspense, and it shows how any consumer would use your product or service. Make sure the demo is ready to go, though. An audience member on stage can be the biggest advocate for or worst critic of your product when he or she sits back down.

When you think of live demonstrations, no other company does the product demonstration quite like Apple. Steve Jobs first revealed FaceTime on the iPhone by calling his friend and colleague Jony Ive. Executing a technological demo successfully can be magical for the audience, but it can harm your credibility if external factors such as spotty WiFi or malfunctioning equipment prevent it. Rehearse, rehearse, rehearse. And always have a backup plan.

Social Media

Creating a hashtag for your presentation is a great way to establish a connection with your audience. It also gives you the ability to track engagement. You can see how many people use the hashtag, how it's shared, and what people are saying. You can measure reach, frequency, and public opinion all by sharing a unique hashtag.

However, hashtags can also hurt you. For example, for its keynote at CES 2013, Qualcomm decided to do an over-the-top presentation with actors, musicians, and guest appearances. While that sounds amazing in theory, its execution confused some viewers watching live and online. They took to Twitter to express their confusion and to poke fun at Qualcomm.

 Ross Miller @ohrnorosco

I think they're about to show sexting on stage at Qualcomm... and still get it very, very wrong.

7 Jan 13

Joshua Topolsky
@joshuatopolsky

NOTHING says Qualcomm like a vampire attack

7 Jan 13

David Pierce
@piercedavid

OMFG BIG BIRD IS HERE I DON'T UNDERSTAND WHAT IS HAPPENING

7 Jan 13

Key takeaway: Make sure the people in your audience are comfortable with what you deliver or be prepared to face their wrath.

Put Your Presentation Online

You can also prompt audience interaction by posting your presentation online on sites such as SlideShare and Prezi. Your audience, as well as other users, can view the presentation, leave comments, or even follow along during the presentation. Using technology to reach and engage your audience may seem distant or impersonal, but it's a modern approach that proves to be effective.

Kenny's Tip

For more information on how to utilize SlideShare, visit http://www.bigfishpresentations.com for a free e-book.

These are just a few ways to involve your audience in your presentation. The topic, audience demographics, audience size, venue, and time will determine the way or the degree to which you may engage with them. When in doubt, check with the event organizer for guidance on what is appropriate.

AFTER THE EXPERIENCE

As you walk offstage after your presentation, you're going to feel both pumped up with adrenaline and relieved that it's over. You've shaken hands, maybe even networked a little. Now is not the time to rest. This is a crucial stage in ensuring the effectiveness of your presentation. The people in your audience may have absorbed your message, and you may have done a great job of engaging them in some kind of dialogue, but all of this means nothing unless you inspire action to be taken.

To do this, you've got to leave your audience with something, whether that is a physical object or the urgency to pursue action. You need to show them that you care about the topic prepresentation and postpresentation. This gives the audience members a direct connection with you. The better the relationship you can form with your audience, the better your chance of creating change. You can use everything from flyers with the relevant URLs and contact information to social media follow-ups and USB drives of your presentation with a link to more collateral. Whatever the leave-behind is, make sure it ties directly into your idea.

If you're an author, speaking at events is a great way to get your book out there. One of our clients, the *New York Times* bestselling author of *New Rules of Marketing and PR* (which we recommend to any aspiring or veteran marketer) and a phenomenal presenter in his own right, David Meerman Scott, spoke at a conference in Buffalo, New York, years ago. While his presentation was delivered wonderfully, Meerman Scott extended the impact of his message by putting a copy of his book into grab bags given to each conference attendee. This helped the audience remember his message and reflect on it in a physical form. They could also share it with others. After all, good books are meant to be shared.

Kenny's Tip

I do three things after every single speech, all of which have resulted in business: (1) I let people know how they can contact me if they enjoyed my presentation. I ask for their cards and send them resources to help them make better presentations. (2) I share my Twitter user name with a hashtag for audience members to tweet their thoughts on my presentation. And (3) I upload my deck to websites such as SlideShare (slideshare.net /bigfishpresentations) and include it as a PDF on our blog page (hookyouraudience.com). When I'm able to record my presentation, I upload it to our YouTube channel and other social networks.

At an *Entrepreneur Magazine* conference in New Orleans, graffiti artist Erik Wahl spoke about standing up to fear. During his presentation, he gave several works of art that he had painted live onstage. This resulted in many tweets about how awesome his paintings were. It got traction on social media and increased the value of his work. At the end of his keynote, he announced a treasure hunt called "Art Drop," saying he would leave beautiful paintings of the icons of a city throughout each city in which he spoke. This prompted the audience to check his social media page at certain times for clues to where he left the paintings. People went crazy when he revealed that the beloved New Orleans Saints quarterback Drew Brees was the subject of one of the paintings up for grabs.

While not every presentation can include complex scavenger hunts, other examples discussed earlier might inspire you to extend the impact of your presentation.

Kenny's Tip

If you have books to share but no way to transport them, have no fear. If you have an e-book edition, give it as a gift to attendees. This is perfect, as it will require the people in your audience to give you their e-mail addresses. Just put their contact info into the "Give a gift" option on Amazon, and they'll receive an electronic redemption code. If you're promoting your book, just make sure you clear it with the event organizer first.

HOW TO GET VALUABLE FEEDBACK

The presentation is finished. Your message was powerful, your slides were gorgeous, and your delivery was engaging. You feel good about everything, and the audience members seemed to enjoy themselves. Some might even want to speak with you afterward. After all the hard work you've put into this, it's time to sit back and relax, right?

Not quite.

After the applause, smiles, and handshakes, you still have some work to do, because it's time for postpresentation feedback.

But what if your presentation was perfect? Why would you need feedback? First of all, no presentation is perfect. In very rare cases, there might be only a small amount of criticism, but you still need feedback. Why? To continue to improve as a presenter, you need to hear the bad as well as the good.

Whether it's a compliment on your slide design or a correction of your pronunciation of a certain word, it's important to know how your presentation was received. Having a group of peers, other speakers, mentors, or select audience members critique your presentation is valuable.

Feedback is key to improvement. You're trying to become a better presenter by enhancing the overall experience for the audience. You're looking for constructive criticism that you can take into consideration for your next presentation.

Try to get as much detailed feedback as possible so that you can address any problems right away. Instead of settling for simple yes-or-no answers, press your audience for specific reasons why your presentation was effective and entertaining—or why it wasn't. "You were good" or "I didn't like it" is practically worthless for improving your presentation skills. "You were good because . . ." or "I didn't like the part when you . . ." is what you are looking for. The more specific the feedback, the better.

Here are a few questions to ask your audience:

- Did I make my main point clear? How?

- Did I ramble too much? When?

- Were my slides confusing? Which ones?

- Did I make you care about my points? In what way?

- How was my delivery? How can I be more natural?

- Did I pause enough, talk too fast, have awkward body movements, or do anything that made you uncomfortable? If so, what?

- What's the biggest thing I can improve on?

- What do I need to keep doing? Why?

Don't take feedback personally. When people tell you they don't like something, don't get defensive. Instead, think of negative feedback as a tool to help you do better next time. Without it, we would all keep making the same mistakes over and over again. Without honesty from audiences, presentations would never improve. Use their criticism to build yourself up, one comment at a time.

Another important part of getting feedback is the process of documenting it for later use. Carry a notepad, pass out comment forms, record audio or video— whatever is most convenient—just make sure you have a system of documentation. Keeping records of all the comments will remind you to incorporate the feedback into your work. As you're preparing for your next presentation, go over the comments a few times. You'll be surprised at not only how much you can learn but also how much you'll remember if you have a record of the feedback.

It's best to get and review feedback immediately after a presentation while it is still fresh in your mind. If you have handwritten notes, transcribe them as soon as you can; it will help you remember the changes you need to make later when you rehearse.

After feedback is given, focus on the most common points. Don't try to tackle too much at once. Over time, these efforts will build on each other, and your skills will drastically improve.

While feedback is extremely valuable, not all of it is necessarily helpful. You have to take each piece of advice with a grain (or a pound) of salt, evaluating it to see if it aligns with the vision you have for your presentation. Advice is free, but taking the wrong kind can cost you. Do what feels right, and disregard what doesn't apply. It takes time and patience to incorporate feedback, but it also requires judgment to determine how efficiently you will improve.

Finding and eliminating weaknesses, as well as capitalizing and expanding upon strengths, is crucial to growing as a speaker. Occasionally you may want to skip the process of getting feedback, but acquiring this valuable information will greatly benefit you in the long run.

CONCLUSION

We've talked about being unique and standing out from the crowd. We've talked about how to conquer the stage, what to do before and after the presentation, and how to engage with your audience. Thinking and talking about these things is one thing, but actually putting all these ideas into practice is quite another.

When it comes to creating an experience for your audience, you have to be very disciplined, diligent, and detail-oriented.

Think back to why you're presenting in the first place. Whether it's trying to spread an idea, raise money, or make people laugh, every presentation has a purpose. Find and remember yours as you craft your presentation experience. It will help you maintain focus along the way, and it will also yield greater results in the end. There is a lot of work that goes into it, from preparation to follow-up, but ultimately you will have inspired a group of people with your ideas and taken the first and most important step toward creating change.

Challenges

NOVICE

- Create a title or headline that's catchy and resonates emotionally with your audience.

- Before your next public presentation, connect with audience members and ask them what they would like to learn from your talk.

- Upload your next presentation on YouTube and SlideShare to promote yourself and to request feedback.

EXPERT

- Give away a creative token during your next presentation (Dima Ghawi gave away a piece of the glass vase she broke onstage to audience members).

- Appeal to four of the five senses in your next presentation.

- Find a way to incorporate audience interaction every 10 minutes, whether it's through a live demo of your technology, activities, or questions.

CONCLUSION: OUR CALL TO ACTION

All good things must come to an end.

We'd like to give you one final call to action: *always present for the greater good of the world.*

Being a great communicator is a gift, and it should be shared and treated like one. Be a force for positive change. We hope that the knowledge we've shared can help accomplish that. Grow that gift.

We at Big Fish Presentations wish you the best of luck on your presentation endeavors and look forward to hearing about how you are using these to change the world.

Happy presenting!

—BIG FISH PRESENTATIONS

Thank you.

EXTRA RESOURCES

Key Presentation Points

THE BIG FISH PRESENTATIONS PROCESS

- Engaging Content + Memorable and Simple Design + Powerful Delivery = Unforgettable Experience for Your Audience

- The 10 Big Fish Presentations Commandments:

  1. Present what's in it for the world, not you.
  2. Remember that time is not a renewable resource; respect it.
  3. Never deliver a presentation you wouldn't want to sit through.
  4. Be aware that people will always remember the presenter more than the presentation.
  5. Be passionate about your topic.
  6. Tell stories.
  7. Always have a progression that leads to a call to action.
  8. If you think you've rehearsed enough, rehearse again.
  9. Engage with the audience when possible.
  10. Have fun.

- All great presenters are confident, optimistic, understanding, realistic, able, genuine, and engaging.

CONTENT

- Before you present, go through the five Ws (who, what, where, when, why) and how.

- Use your research to come up with an overarching concept that makes the audience think and feel rather than just watch.

- The big idea is the purpose of the presentation.

- If you can't say what your presentation is about in one sentence, you're doing something wrong.

- Craft three main points and supporting material for each.

- Be creative in your opener: tell stories, ask questions, recite quotes, share statistics, or tell a joke.

- There are three main elements to a compelling story: the emotional content and context of the story, the villain (problem) and the hero (the audience), and the suspense.

- When dealing with data, present it in a relevant, purposeful, and emotional way to make it relatable for the audience.

- Every presentation needs a call to action that creates tangible change by asking a hard-hitting question, making a powerful demand, or offering a solution.

- Prime the audience with a road map of your presentation verbally and visually—and stick to it.

- Use words and phrases that aren't only memorable but also shareable in conversation and through social media.

- Adding content to your presentation is easy. The real trick is to take away what is extraneous, leaving a simple and powerful message.

DESIGN

- The first step in design is to create a storyboard.

- Evaluate, ideate, and refine until your concepts are strong enough to be fleshed out.

- What makes a good slide? Simple. Understandable. Memorable.

- Color has psychological meaning. Use it to evoke emotion.

- Design with a hierarchy in mind. This involves color, alignment, scale, weight, and spatial intervals.

- When designing slides, use minimal text, powerful photography, and easily readable fonts and take advantage of white space.

- Avoid clichéd stock photography at all costs. Be relatable.

- Animation and videos help to show process, to compare and contrast, and to build up to a big reveal.

- Go beyond cold, hard data and show what it means to the audience through creative graphs, charts, and infographics.

- Printed handouts can be effective marketing pieces in addition to providing supplemental information.

- Printed handouts can also be distracting. Their distribution should be timed carefully.

- PowerPoint isn't your only presentation option. Experiment with other platforms, depending on your audience.

DELIVERY

- There are four different delivery styles: teacher, host, coach, headliner. Which one are you?

- Know your time limit and go under it.

- Good body language means genuine facial expressions, strong eye contact, natural gestures, and open postures.

- Don't talk too fast or you'll lose your audience. Don't talk too slow or you'll put your audience to sleep. Balance your energy.

- Slow down. Breathe. Think. Your audience will appreciate it.

- If you're thinking about saying "um" or "you know," pause to find the right words.

- Feedback is more important than you think. Prepare for the future by studying the past.

- Anything can be interesting. Sell the sizzle, not the steak.

- When rehearsing, focus on three things: practicing in real time, timing yourself, and getting feedback.

- Webinars are a great way to connect with audiences online.

EXPERIENCE

- Stage fright is completely normal. Combat it effectively by finding a ritual that puts you at ease.

- Don't be afraid to do something different if the situation allows it.

- Craft a catchy, memorable title and promote your presentation online.

- Keep your audience engaged with activities, questions, and captivating technology.

- After your presentation, follow up to maintain a meaningful connection with your audience.

- Always ask for feedback and incorporate it in your next presentation.

Tools and Inspiration

CONTENT

- *Copyblogger.* E-books and articles on good copy (http://copyblogger.com)

- *Grammar Girl.* Quick, easy grammar tips (http://quickanddirtytips.com)

- *Hubspot.* A compilation of e-books about how to create engaging copy (http://library.hubspot.com)

STORYBOARDING/BRAINSTORMING

- *Fifty Three Paper.* A great app that allows you to sketch out slides on your iPad (https://www.fiftythree.com/paper)

- *Wordstorm.* A website that enables you to find words that relate to your topic (http://www.lonij.net/wordstorm/wordstorm.php)

DESIGN

- *Prezi.* A zooming, nonlinear presentation design tool (http://prezi.com)

- *SlideShare.* A social media network that shares trending slide shows (http://slideshare.net)

- *Haiku Deck.* An online editor that helps designers and nondesigners alike create easy slide decks on the go (http://haikudeck.com)

- *Scrollmotion.* A mobile presentation application perfect for training, educational, and sales presentations (http://scrollmotion.com)

- *Bunkr.* An html-based presentation design tool (http://bunkr.me)

- *Flowvella.* An interactive online presentation tool that allows you to organize content into sections (http://flowboard.com)

- *Projeqt.* Made by ad agency TBWA, a presentation design tool that integrates live social media interaction within the presentation (http://projeqt.com)

- *Spritesapp.* Interactive infographics (https://spritesapp.com)

- *Canva.* Easy online photo editor (https://www.canva.com)

- *HowDesign.* A collection of design resources on photography, typography, and other creative media (http://howdesign.com/resources-education)

- *Behance.* A showcase of some of the web's most creative work (http://behance.com)

- *Design Hunt.* A curated selection of trending design tools and tricks (http://www.talkaboutdesign.com)

- *Type Genius.* A website where you can, in its own words, "find the perfect font combo for your next project" (http://www.typegenius.com)

- *SlideRocket.* A tool that gets you better feedback on team slides (http://www.sliderocket.com)

- *Sway.* Microsoft's online presentation/website editor with easily embedded interactive media (http://www.sway.com)

- *Deckset.* Instant content to slide deck for presenters in a rush (http://www.decksetapp.com)

- *Note and Point.* A collection of some of the best-designed presentations in PowerPoint and Keynote (http://www.noteandpoint.com)

- *Piktochart.* Infographics (http://piktochart.com)

- *Visual.ly.* A marketplace for presentations, infographics, and motion graphic videos (http://visual.ly)

- *Fonts in Use.* Free designer fonts (http://fontsinuse.com)

- *Font Squirrel.* Free designer fonts (http://fontsquirrel.com)

- *Lost Type.* A collection of available-for-purchase designer fonts (http://losttype.com)

- *Urbanfont.* Free designer fonts (http://urbanfont.com)

- *Public Domain Archive.* Free stock photos (http://publicdomainarchive.com)

- *iStock.* Royalty-free photos (http://istock.com)

- *Shutterstock.* Royalty-free photos (http://shutterstock.com)

- *Airstoc.* Aerial stock photos (https://www.airstoc.com)

- *Offset.* A more expensive option for premium stock photos and illustrations (http://offset.com)

- *Facebox.* Inexpensive stock photos of faces (http://facebox.io)

- *Placeit.* Website that lets you quickly place screenshots of photos into frames (http://placeit.net)

- *Awwwards.* A collection of some of the web's best digital design (http://awwwards.com)

DELIVERY/EXPERIENCE

- *TED.* TED talks (http://ted.com)

- *99u.* Inspiring talks (http://99u.com/videos)

- *NPR Commencement.* A collection of the best commencement speeches (http://apps.npr.org/commencement)

MISCELLANEOUS

- *Kivo.* An annotative tool that enables others to give feedback on your PowerPoint decks (https://www.kivo.com)

- *Tweetwall.* A platform that allows you to display your hashtag at your event; can be used on-screen during a presentation (http://tweetwall.com)

- *Slidedog.* A tool that lets you create a seamless playlist of presentations, perfect for conferences (http://slidedog.com)

- *Producthunt.* A curated selection of the latest software, technology, and overall cool stuff. Monitor this website for new presentation software and tools (http://www.producthunt.com)

- *Catchbox.* A box containing a microphone that can spark activity-driven discussions (http://us.getcatchbox.com)

Books

FOR CONTENT AND DELIVERY

- *Made to Stick* by Chip Heath and Dan Heath

- *Presenting to Win* by Jerry Weissman

- *Resonate* by Nancy Duarte

- *HBR Guide to Persuasive Presentations* by Nancy Duarte

- *How to Deliver a TED Talk* by Jeremey Donovan

- *Confessions of a Public Speaker* by Scott Berkun

- *Pitch Anything* by Oren Klaff

- *Presentation Secrets of Steve Jobs* by Carmine Gallo

- *Talk Like TED* by Carmine Gallo

FOR DESIGN

- *Presentation Zen* by Garr Reynolds

- *Presentation Zen Design* by Garr Reynolds

- *Slide:ology* by Nancy Duarte

- *Infographics* by Column Five

- *Thinking with Type* by Ellen Lupton

- *The Back of a Napkin* by Dan Roam

- *Graphic Design* by Ellen Lupton

NOTES

CHAPTER 2

1. Anne Fisher, *Conquering the Five-Minute Attention Span*, http://fortune.com/2013/07/10/giving-a-speech-conquer-the-five-minute-attention-span/.
2. Carol Goman, *Seven Seconds to Make a First Impression*, http://www.forbes.com/sites/carolkinseygoman/2011/02/13/seven-seconds-to-make-a-first-impression/.
3. Carmine Gallo, *The Presentation Secrets of Steve Jobs*, page 110.
4. Doug Pray, documentary: *Art & Copy*.

CHAPTER 3

1. The Apple Special Event, http://www.apple.com/apple-events/september-2013/.
2. From the YouTube video, http://www.youtube.com/watch?v=t3mAHQuBqQI.
3. Nancy Duarte, *HBR Guide to Persuasive Presentations*.
4. Garr Reynolds, *Presentation Zen*, Volume 1.
5. Scott Gerber, *10 Tips for Company Color Schemes*, http://mashable.com/2013/06/09/color-schemes-business/.
6. Ellen Lupton and Jennifer Cole Phillips, *Graphic Design: The New Basics* (Princeton: Princeton Architectural Press, 2008).
7. Karen Haller, *Colour Psychology . . . The Meaning of Green*, http://karenhaller.co.uk/blog/colour-psychology-the-meaning-of-green.
8. Karen Haller, *Business Branding Colours . . . The Meaning of Green*, http://karenhaller.co.uk/blog/business-branding-colours%E2%80%A6-meaning-of-green/.
9. Karen Haller, *Colour Psychology . . . The Meaning of Yellow*, http://karenhaller.co.uk/blog/colour-psychology%E2%80%A6-the-meaning-of-yellow/.
10. Karen Haller, *Colour Psychology . . . The Meaning of Red*, http://karenhaller.co.uk/blog/wp-content/uploads/2012/02/Colour-Psychology-the-meaning-of-red-red-signs.jpg.
11. Michelle Manetti, *America's Favorite Color Is Blue, According to House Beautiful's 2012 Color Report*, http://www.huffingtonpost.com/2012/08/29/house-beautiful-2012-color-report_n_1840383.html.
12. Karen Haller, *Colour Psychology . . . The Meaning of Brown*, http://karenhaller.co.uk/blog/colour-psychology-the-meaning-of-brown/.
13. Ibid.
14. Karen Haller, *Colour Psychology . . . The Meaning of Black*, http://karenhaller.co.uk/blog/colour-psychology-the-meaning-of-black.
15. Laurence Lessig, *Free Culture* presentation, https://archive.org/details/Lessig-Free_Culture.
16. Karen Haller, *Colour Psychology . . . The Meaning of Orange*, http://karenhaller.co.uk/blog/colour-psychology-%E2%80%A6-the-meaning-of-orange/.
17. Karen Haller, *Colour Psychology . . . The Meaning of Pink*, http://karenhaller.co.uk/blog/colour-psychology-the-meaning-of-pink/.
18. Karen Haller, *Business Branding Colour . . . The Meaning of Blue*, http://karenhaller.co.uk/blog/business-branding-colour-%E2%80%A6-meaning-of-blue/.

19. Harwish Manwani, *Profit's Not Always the Point*, http://www .ted.com/talks/harish_manwani_profit_s_not_always_the _point.html.

20. Ellen Lupton and Jennifer Cole Phillips, *Graphic Design: The New Basics*.

21. Ibid.

22. Ellen Lupton, *Thinking with Type*.

23. Ian Sample, *Higgs Boson: It's Unofficial! Cern Scientists Discover Missing Particle*, http://www.theguardian.com/science/2012 /jul/04/higgs-boson-cern-scientists-discover.

24. SlideShare.net.

25. From the vimeo video, https://vimeo.com/112727142.

26. offset.com.

27. uifaces.com.

28. placeit.net.

29. Garr Reynolds, *From Golden Mean to "Rule of Thirds,"* http:// www.presentationzen.com/presentationzen/2005/08/from _golden_mea.html.

30. http://mariodelvalle.github.io/CaptainIconWeb/.

31. http://iconion.com/.

32. David McCandless, *The Beauty of Data Visualization*, http:// www.ted.com/talks/david_mccandless_the_beauty_of_data _visualization#t-103437.

33. Visually, *What Is an Infographic?*, http://visual.ly/what-is-an -infographic.

34. Alexei Kapterev, *Death by PowerPoint*, http://www.slideshare .net/thecroaker/death-by-powerpoint.

35. Dylan Love, *Steve Job's Favorite Piece of Software Is Now a Cult Hit with Designers*. http://www.businessinsider.com /apple-designed-keynote-with-keynote-2012-10.

36. prezi.com.

37. http://www.crunchbase.com/organization/bunkr.

38. Romain Dillet, *Bunkr Is the PowerPoint Killer We've All Been Waiting For*, http://techcrunch.com/2013/08/22/bunkr-is -the-powerpoint-killer-weve-all-been-waiting-for/.

39. kivo.com.

40. Slidedog.com.

41. tweetwall.com.

42. Freddie Dawson's *How Playing with Kinect Could Lead To The Death Of Powerpoint*, http://www.forbes.com/sites /freddiedawson/2014/05/30/how-playing-with-kinect -could-lead-to-the-death-of-powerpoint/.

CHAPTER 4

1. http://dictionary.reference.com/browse/disfluency.

2. National Institute of Mental Health's *Fear/Phobia Statistics*, http://www.statisticbrain.com/fear-phobia-statistics/.

3. Josh Shosky, *How to Speak Like Churchill*, http://www .totalpolitics.com/campaigns/4698/how-to-speak-like -churchill.thtml.

4. Carmine Gallo, *How Warren Buffett and Joel Osteen Conquered Their Terrifying Fear of Public Speaking*, http://www .forbes.com/sites/carminegallo/2013/05/16/how-warren -buffett-and-joel-osteen-conquered-their-terrifying-fear-of -public-speaking/.

5. Richard Branson, *Art of Public Speaking*, http://www.entrepreneur.com/article/225627.

6. History Central, "Quick Facts About Eleanor Roosevelt," http://www.historycentral.com/ladies/ae_roosevelt.html.

7. TJ Walker, *Conquer Public Speaking Fears the Jay Leno Way*, http://www.tjwalker.com/2013/10/22/conquer-public -speaking-fears-the-jay-leno-way-fear-of-public-speaking/.

8. Carmine Gallo, *How Warren Buffett and Joel Osteen Conquered Their Terrifying Fear of Public Speaking*, http://www .forbes.com/sites/carminegallo/2013/05/16/how-warren -buffett-and-joel-osteen-conquered-their-terrifying-fear-of -public-speaking/.

9. Bradford Evans, *The Pre-Show Rituals of Comedians Just Before They Go on Stage*, http://splitsider.com/2012/09/the-pre -show-rituals-of-comedians-just-before-they-go-on-stage/.

INDEX

ABOUT THE AUTHORS

 **KENNY NGUYEN** is the founder and CEO of Big Fish Presentations, a company whose mantra is "turning presentations into experiences." Kenny and his team work daily with clients nationwide, from startups to Fortune 100 companies, providing high-quality presentation design, presentation training, and creative video production. He was named the 2012 CEO Student Entrepreneur of the Year by Collegiate Entrepreneurs Organization (CEO). Under his leadership, Big Fish Presentations was recognized as one of the top 50 student-led startups in the world by the Kairos Society and one of *Inc. Magazine*'s "Coolest College Start-Ups of 2012." Kenny has been featured in popular news outlets such as *Forbes*, *Entrepreneur Magazine*, *Yahoo*, *Business Insider*, *Mashable*, the *Huffington Post*, and the *Washington Post*. He has spoken at TEDxLSU and HubSpot Inbound and has taught presentation workshops at General Assembly. A curator of 99u Baton Rouge, he is a member of AIGA New Orleans and the host of the online cooking channel You've Got Meal. Kenny is passionate about helping his home city of Baton Rouge become a hub for creative talent in the South. He dreams of owning a corgi one day.

 **GUS MURILLO** is the cofounder, president, and COO of Big Fish Presentations. Since he and Kenny attended the "worst presentation they had ever seen" together, they have been working to rid the world of such experiences. His work at Big Fish includes producing and directing commercial videos. Before graduating from Louisiana State University with a degree in biological sciences, he was recognized as a Kairos50 member for his innovative college startup and was awarded for this achievement at the New York Stock Exchange.

ROBERT KILLEEN is the lead copywriter and creative director at Big Fish Presentations. He has been writing his entire life—short stories and fake TV scripts that will never see the light of day, journals that are best kept private, and blog posts for public consumption. This, however, is his first book. He has a bachelor's degree in mass communication from Louisiana State University and serves as Student Outreach Committee Chair for the American Advertising Federation of Baton Rouge and Marketing Coordinator for 99u Local: Baton Rouge.

LUKE JONES has the distinction of being the first copywriter of Big Fish Presentations. He is now a copywriting associate at DEVENEY Communication. A born entrepreneur, he started a T-shirt company and a neighborhood newspaper in his youth. He has worked at production studios, design firms, and advertising agencies. Luke received his bachelor's degree in mass communication from Louisiana State University. He loves words, movies, cream soda, and his miniature schnauzer, Albus—not necessarily in that order.

Visit us at:

bigfishpresentations.com   facebook.com/bigfishpresco/   youtube.com/user/BigFishpresentations

@BigFishPresCo   slideshare.net/bigfishpresentations   prezi.com/user/bigfishpresentations/prezis/

Linked in linkedin.com/company/big-fish-presentations